MUSIC

A JOY FOR LIFE

—

Sir Edward Heath

Edward Heath

CLASSIC *f*M

—

EDWARD HEATH

—

MUSIC
A JOY FOR LIFE

FOREWORD BY
YEHUDI MENUHIN

PAVILION

Acknowledgements

Edward Greenfield, Richard Baker, Michael Bukht, Robert O'Dowd,

Christopher Joyce, Minor Myers Jr, Michael McManus, Colin Webb, Anne Askwith

First published in Great Britain in 1997 by
Pavilion Books Limited
26 Upper Ground, London SE1 9PD

Text copyright © Edward Heath 1976, 1997

Designed by Nigel Partridge

A CIP catalogue record for this book is available from the British Library

ISBN 1 86205 090 2

Typeset in Perpetua

Printed in Great Britain by The Cromwell Press, Melksham
2 4 6 8 10 9 7 5 3 1

This book may be ordered by post direct from the publisher.
Please contact the Marketing Department.
But try your bookshop first

CONTENTS

FOREWORD

———

'A man who has no music *in himself,* nor is moved with concord of sweet sounds, is fit for treasons, stratagems and spoils.' How imperative it is, therefore, that, of all professions, it is politicians who should ideally 'carry music in themselves', from their earliest days, so that, attuned to song and through singing, they should have learnt to listen – to listen to others and eventually to that still small voice in their own hearts which is so often drowned in the business of living; to remember; and through memory of sounds, to make into one the realms of thought and emotion. Edward Heath had this 'joy for life', which is music, from his earliest years. I firmly believe that it is in infancy that the seeds of a benign and happy old age are planted.

My most particular recollections of Ted are those of musical occasions, such as when he invited the children and staff of my school to Chequers, when affairs of state were suspended and all hearts spoke, not least when Ted established his credentials as a colleague by performing a Handel sonata with me. The children played beautifully, as is their wont, and were fascinated and delighted when warned not to touch the red telephone in the bedroom as it was the direct line to the heads of state in Moscow and Washington, which I am sure they might have used to purposes more innocent and transparent than many an elder.

There followed a few days later a letter from Margaret Thatcher – then Minister of Education – offering the Yehudi Menuhin School the support of the state. It was the first music school to be granted this lifeline – surely one of the most enlightened and far-sighted decisions ever taken by any government! Other such schools soon followed – all with the ideal of producing well-balanced human beings capable of thought, compassion and decision, and that synoptic view of life which music offers.

Yet another cherished memory of Ted is the celebration at Downing Street of Sir William Walton's seventieth birthday. Never was a celebration more perfectly and affectionately conceived; the music which preceded, punctuated and closed the evening, as well as every item, including the menu, were exquisitely chosen, and the words ushering the players and music were on the most cultivated level of this most civilized man.

Nor will I ever forget the commitment Ted showed on the podium when, baton in hand, he conducted the Brahms Double Concerto with a very fine cellist from my school, Felix Schmidt, and myself as soloists. Those were among the manifold qualities which revealed Edward Heath beyond the bounds of statesman or politician, as a man who, speaking of the 'unacceptable face of capitalism', could truly recognize that however beneficial a theory, it also carries within it the limits that might prove harmful. That he also revels in the other English loves of nature, the wind, the sea and the land is crystallized in that lovely house in the Close of Salisbury Cathedral. This completes the image of a man to whom I am particularly devoted and with whom I share visions, ideas and convictions.

As a colleague I salute him with real affection and admiration.

YEHUDI MENUHIN

INTRODUCTION

───

Beethoven wrote on the score of his *Missa Solemnis:* 'it is from the heart, may it go to the heart', and this inscription could speak for the whole of music. I have listened to, and loved, music for as long as I can remember. For performers, conductors and listeners, music transcends all boundaries of language, politics and culture. At its best, music is the purest and most moving form of art, and I hope that this book will, as its subtitle suggests, enable me to share with the reader some of the joy and unique inspiration that music can bring.

I hope too that I can pass on to a younger generation memories of musical traditions in Britain that are lost or forgotten; that I shall encourage some people to try classical music, and others to sample new works and new composers for the first time; and that I shall also encourage people to seek out some of the finest recordings that I have come across in some sixty years of listening, for there are few better ways of learning and enjoying a wider repertoire.

Since the first edition of this book was published in 1976, music has continued to give me joy, not just as a listener, but as a performer as well – I have rather reduced my concert-going, but in place of listening I have had the privilege of conducting many of the world's greatest orchestras, on a variety of continents. This all really began with a performance of Sir Edward Elgar's 'Cockaigne' Overture in November 1971, when, as Prime Minister, I conducted the London Symphony Orchestra. Since that time the list of works and orchestras that I have conducted has certainly expanded dramatically, but it is still often to that piece that I return. I always find that its inspired themes, its magnificent orchestrations and its unequalled evocation of London place it amongst the great English works.

Last July I celebrated my eightieth birthday with a series of parties for my friends and a series of five symphony concerts, beginning in late May with the Oxford Orchestra da Camera at the Sheldonian Theatre in Oxford, moving on in July to a *Schloß* in southern Germany, to Salisbury Cathedral, to Kenwood, and then finally with the BBC to the Hippodrome in Golders Green. The last work on that final programme was none other than 'Cockaigne' – and the BBC Concert Orchestra, like the LSO twenty-five years earlier, rose to the occasion with style. The performers were different, the audience was different and the world had moved on – but this marvellous work, and the values it still represents, remained every bit as moving and powerful as ever. Meanwhile, the live recording of that 1971 performance was made available on CD for the first time.

The pleasure that these birthday concerts gave me reminded me only too well that for me music continues to be a true joy for life, and I sincerely hope that this book will imprint some of that joy to my readers, and will inspire them to enrich their lives through the unique qualities that only music possesses.

EDWARD HEATH

Salisbury, 1996

CHAPTER ONE

EARLY JOYS

——

My father used to say to me when I got sick to death of playing scales and arpeggios, particularly on summer evenings when other attractions loomed large in a boy's life: 'Stick to it! Once you've mastered it, nobody can ever take it away from you. Your music will be a joy for life.' At that time this did not seem much of a consolation. It wasn't far to cycle to the beach for a swim, or to the vicarage garden for tennis with the parish youth club – and those grinding scales and arpeggios became ever more complicated as one got further and further into the finger exercises. Would they never come to an end? One of the lessons I had to learn then applies to so many other things in life as well: the ultimate result depends on a mastery of technique, or rather, the best generally cannot be obtained without that technique. And technique is something that has to be maintained throughout life. In his final judgement my father was absolutely right: as you absorb music, so it becomes part of your life. It can't be taken away from you.

I did not come from a particularly musical family, though we quite frequently had music in the home. Both my father and mother were children of large families, most of whose members still lived in the village of St Peter's-in-Thanet, or in the seaside town of Broadstairs near by, and they all kept closely in touch. When, on Saturday or Sunday evening, my brother and I went as children to visit them, the grown-ups would often gather round the piano, after some coffee and sandwiches, to sing. It made a break from playing whist or rummy, card games which bored both my brother and me. The songs they sang were Victorian, or at the latest Edwardian, but they still formed the repertoire customary on such occasions in the twenties and thirties. Indeed, as a Member of Parliament, I still hear them sung today, seventy years later, at gatherings where old-age pensioners and other groups are being entertained by local singers who certainly know well the tastes of their listeners.

'Roses of Picardy' and 'Love's Old Sweet Song' were firm favourites. My father, who had a light tenor voice, usually contributed an English version of an aria from Verdi's *Il Trovatore*, *'Ah, che la morte'*, commonly rendered as 'Ah! I have sigh'd to rest me'. The meaning of this was not entirely clear to me, but it was a good tune. It has, however, had a long-enduring effect, which has prevented me from enjoying that work of Verdi's, for whenever we reach the point where Manrico slides into this aria against the background chanting of the *'Miserere'* I find myself once again mentally 'sighing to rest me' and I want to break into hysterical laughter. Almost always the sessions came to an end with Arthur Sullivan's 'The Lost Chord', followed by 'When you come to the end of a perfect day'. These were obviously not works of any great significance, but as light music they served their purpose well and the quality of their craftsmanship was high. Not only could they be sung by distinguished vocalists at social functions, a mayor's banquet or a society's annual dinner, but the family could also sing and play them in the home and gain satisfaction from them. It was a time when radio was still in the process of establishing itself and before television had appeared. We had to make our own entertainment, and this was a natural way of doing so. In modern terms it was 'participation', though nobody ever dreamed of calling it that. Only my grandparents sat back in their chairs and listened, some-times criticizing or occasionally applauding; for the rest of us, to stand round the piano and sing was the thing to do.

The pianist on these occasions was almost always an aunt on my mother's side. She played well and occasionally invited me to her small home in Margate, where I sometimes succeeded in getting her to sit down at the piano and play for me. She usually played the popular works of the time, hardly ever those of the classical masters. 'Autumn' by Charminade produced a lovely melody with the rustling of the leaves in the accompaniment, a rather wintry storm and the final fall of the leaves from the trees. Durand's First Valse – somewhat reminiscent of Chopin's 'Minute Waltz' – was whisked off at a tremendous pace though with a sentimental interlude in the middle. Paderewski's Minuet gave her an opportunity to explain to me how this simple, catchy work had been composed by a man who was not only one of the greatest pianists of his day but had also been Prime Minister of his country.

My favourite, for which I always asked at the end of these personal recitals, was Grieg's 'Wedding day at Troldhaugen'. How beautifully it evokes the atmosphere of the scenes he is depicting; the clip-clop of the ponies' hooves as they draw the sleigh of the bridal couple to the church, a cheerful theme for the occasion building up over them, chords crash-ing out from one end of the piano to the other as the bells ring out for the arrival of the bride at the church door. Inside all is hushed; we lis-ten to the organ quietly playing through the service. Then the bride and bridegroom are borne away; more bells, the sound of hooves gradually fading far into the distance until the piece is brought to an end with the usual thunderous chord. That was the one I liked best and I wanted to be able to play it myself. Today it is largely forgotten, like most of Grieg's music except for the Suite from *Peer Gynt* and the Piano Concerto. It used to be possible to get it on a record by Arthur de Greef, the acknowledged authority at that time on Grieg's Piano Concerto. Even in the CD age, this recording has still not been restored to the catologue.

Seeing how keen I was and sensing that I might have some talent, my aunt urged my parents to let me learn the piano. The problem was how to get an instrument on which to learn. My parents had only just returned to St Peter's from Crayford, some twenty miles south-east of London, where they had gone to live in the middle of the First World War, six months after I was born, so that my father could work on building aircraft in the Vickers factory there. He was now foreman on a building site for a local contractor. He was renting our house and to buy a piano in these circumstances was no mean undertaking. But both my parents wanted to encourage me and were prepared to make sacrifices to do so. Eventually they decided to commit themselves to buying a new instrument and one Saturday afternoon we set off to the main music shop in Margate, Thornton Bobby, a shop well known in the area for its range of musical equipment. We looked at a variety of pianos and listened to what the salesman had to say about them. Finally, relying very largely on the manager's judgement and advice, my father agreed to buy a piano made specially for Thornton Bobby and sold under their own name. My aunt, who was with us, thought it had a good touch – something in pianos to which I have learned to attach importance – and also considered that it would wear well. It certainly did, for it remained in our home for forty years. The price was £42, to be paid in twenty-four monthly instalments. It was a good buy and it made an exciting present on my ninth birthday.

The local music teacher was Miss Locke, the daughter of the man who

kept the flower shop opposite the parish church. She agreed to teach me
and to come to the house once a week throughout the year to give me
an hour's lesson. She was insistent, however, that I would have to take it
seriously and practise regularly every evening between her weekly
lessons; she relied on my parents to see that this was carried out. Thus
began the hours of learning how to finger scales, each hand singly, both
hands together, scales of every type and range and sweeping arpeggios
covering a scale with three leaps at a time. These were combined with
elementary pieces, usually those set for examinations by the musical
authorities. As I worked at these basic tasks, Grieg's 'Wedding Day'
seemed a long way away. Gradually, however, I began to embark on
works that gave me, musically, more satisfaction. I was always in too
much of a hurry and became impatient with Miss Locke's insistence that
I should get each piece technically correct before I moved on to another.
What I was after was the musical experience, the opportunity to express
feeling and emotion in pieces of different kinds, according to my moods.
I wasn't always so bothered about making sure that every note came out
exactly as it was intended by the composer. I was more intent upon finding an outlet for my own inner fantasies. If there was one gap at this stage
in my musical understanding, it was a failure to relate all the work I was
doing on scales and other aspects of technique to the pieces I was then
starting to play. If I had fully realized then that this was necessary in
order to master the works on which even at that time my heart was set,
I might have been a little less liable to become enraged by the sheer
drudgery of it all.

I was nine when I started to learn the piano; I was forty-nine when I
began sailing seriously. It would be difficult to find a more complete contrast in approach to two aspects of my life that have given me such

satisfaction. Curiously enough, on one occasion a stranger approached me with a request for me to sign his copy of my book on sailing, which he had been given for Christmas, and when I asked him whether he'd enjoyed it, he replied: 'Yes, and as a result I've taken up learning the piano.'

'Reading *Sailing* led you to take up the piano?' I asked somewhat incredulously.

'Yes,' he replied, 'I had always wanted to play the piano but I was too intimidated to do anything about it. I thought at my age I would look silly. After I had read your book I said to myself "If he can start sailing at forty-nine, there's no reason why I shouldn't start learning the piano at forty-one." My daughter's eleven and she wanted to learn as well, so now we learn together. We keep each other up to the mark, though I must say,' he added rather ruefully, 'it is a bit difficult at times to keep up with her.'

I was delighted. Of course he was right. I have known much older people who have begun to learn to play an instrument, often a piano or an electronic organ. If you can do it within the family, so much the better. It is not a question of getting to the point where you can show off to the neighbours, let alone play in public or become a concert pianist. It is a means of self-expression, of understanding more about the music to which you listen, of giving yourself pleasure in your home. For those who are attracted to the organ there is always the possibility of being able to fill an empty organ stool in the local parish church. In many villages today, the vicar or minister has a problem finding someone who can play regularly for the services. Such a post also provides an opportunity for training and building up a choir as well as leading congregational singing. I know of few things more worthwhile, both for organist and congregation, than full-throated, though musically under-standing, singing in the body of the kirk.

It was a fact of English musical life that practically every leading composer, conductor, organist or music administrator received his basic grounding in church music. The Salvation Army too has contributed to the training of other musicians, in particular wind instrumentalists; two trumpet-playing contemporaries of mine at grammar school, both of whom learned their instruments in the local Salvation Army band, later went on to become first and second trumpets in the BBC Symphony Orchestra. In the nineteenth century it was the cathedral organists who not only played for the services and trained the choir, but also themselves wrote much of the music. In addition, they usually conducted the local choral society, which was accompanied either by an amateur orchestra or by one of the provincial orchestras brought in for festival occasions.

I was fortunate enough both to learn the piano from an early age and to learn about singing. After an audition with the organist Alfred Tattam I was accepted as a chorister at St Peter's-in-Thanet and told that I would be expected to attend the boys' rehearsals on Tuesday evenings, a complete choir rehearsal on Fridays, and Matins and Evensong on Sundays. Once a month I would also be expected to sing at Choral Communion and from time to time there would be special occasions such as weddings and funerals at which the choir would be required. The financial remuneration would be a penny halfpenny for each practice and twopence halfpenny on Sundays – old pence, of course. The total sum would be paid at the end of every three months. I should add that weddings – though not funerals – were sometimes more remunerative, and when the daughter of the local doctor in Broadstairs got married, not only were we paid half a crown each for singing at the service but the whole choir was invited to the reception afterwards. For us, that was an unforgettable occasion.

In the choir in St Peter's-in-Thanet we were brought up on a musical diet that must have been typical of most parish churches fifty years ago. It was a well-balanced choir of some twenty-four boys and twelve men. The organist was a good choir trainer who, at the same time, believed strongly in giving a lead on the organ that would produce bold congregational singing. The anthems on Sunday mornings tended to be of two kinds. On the one hand, there were the individual pieces taken from major choral works by Handel, Haydn, Mozart and Mendelssohn; on the other, there were anthems typical of the English church composers of the time. Many of these are still sung in our churches and cathedrals.

At Christmas and Easter we had the opportunity of a change. The carol service on the Sunday evening after Christmas consisted of two or three groups of well-known carols, almost entirely taken from Novello's collection. The *Oxford Carol Book,* with its wide variety of carols from many countries, some of them in splendid harmonizations, had not then made its impact on church choirs. Nor had the form of service on Christmas Eve at King's College, Cambridge, become as widely known as it is today as a result of being broadcast on radio and television. One work was always included so long as we had our splendid baritone soloist Mr Boardman with us. That was *Nazareth,* composed by Charles Gounod. How well he used to develop that flowing, melodic line! 'Though poor be the chamber,' he vibrated. With what emotion did we choristers answer him in the choruses! We were all terrified of him. He was a broad-shouldered, well-built man who never disguised his views when he thought the choir unworthy of his performance. Nor did he ever hesitate to chide us in an attempt to get us to perform better.

At Easter we normally performed one major work on the evening of Good Friday. It was for many years Sir John Stainer's *Crucifixion,* a simple work hardly ever heard today, but one which when well sung can still be effective. Later we turned to a weightier and more complex work, Gounod's *Redemption,* which proved much more difficult to master. Later still we sang *The Passion according to St Luke,* sometimes attributed to Bach, much shorter and simpler than either the St Matthew or St John Passion. I have never understood by what authority this work has been attributed to Johann Sebastian Bach but it certainly provided a contrast to both Stainer's *Crucifixion* and Gounod's *Redemption.*

St Peter's-in-Thanet must have been one of the first churches to change over completely to the English Hymnal. Perhaps it was because the vicar at the time, the Reverend C.H.S. Mathews, was a remarkable man who, after spending some of his earlier years in Australia, had returned with the reputation of being a forceful preacher and something of a radical. The English Hymnal gave us the opportunity of appreciating straight away some splendid new hymn tunes, in particular Vaughan Williams's magnificent setting of 'For All the Saints', surely one of the finest ever written. Yet one thing always puzzled me about this, or rather about the words to which it was set. Time and again, as a boy, I sang:

> Through gates of pearl streams
> In the countless host

I long wondered what 'pearl streams' were. No one ever bothered to alter our breathing and punctuation in those lines so that the countless host were made to stream in through gates of pearl! A small point, but perhaps it emphasizes how important it is to make sure that singers understand the meaning of the words they are mouthing. Only then can they have any hope of putting real colour, light and shade and spirit into their performance.

The knowledge of church music that I was imbibing at this time was supplemented by the performances of the Broadstairs Choral Society, a local body of some sixty to eighty singers, which gave one or two performances a year, with orchestra. While I was still a chorister there was no place for me in such a body, but I was usually invited to sell programmes at the concerts. As a result of being at these performances, and the rehearsals for them, I became intrigued by the whole process of conducting. It seemed to me that having control over a choir and orchestra, shaping them to produce the sound one wanted, having soloists singing out of one's hand, so to speak, was really something worthwhile. I was quite soon to become involved.

My voice broke. I moved from the lower to the upper choir stalls and began to sing in a rather limited baritone voice, never quite reaching a tenor register with any ease, nor having the resonance to sink to the depths of a true bass. Nevertheless, I was able to take part in all the choral work we were then doing, as well as to join in singing madrigals and part-songs in groups that used to meet in a few people's homes.

What a pity it is that all too seldom now we gather in each other's homes for this purpose, especially as so much of this music was written by our own composers. Many of those who sang madrigals and part-songs together formed the nucleus of a mixed-voice choir, which competed regularly in the musical festivals that were a feature of our area. The founder having decided to move to a rather warmer part of the south coast, I was invited to become their conductor. I was now sixteen and welcomed the opportunity to take responsibility for a choir of some thirty sopranos and altos, tenors and basses. We continued to take part in the festivals and, though I was by far the youngest of any of those taking part, we had considerable success. Indeed, although many of the members of the Broadstairs Glee Club, as it was called, had wide experience of this sort of musical activity, they seemed to respond to being led by one so young and to take a pride in it.

After my voice broke, I also started to learn the organ at the parish church. The organ itself was an example of a solid, well-balanced instrument, built by Walker, with what is termed a 'tracker action'. This means that the key is pressed down by the weight of the finger without mechanical assistance. The more stops that are out, the heavier the pressure required. As it had three manuals, or keyboards, and each could be coupled, or interconnected, the pressure required when playing with full organ was quite considerable. On the other hand, this form of action required a clean finger technique. Nothing on the keyboard could be smudged. Unless one's finger was pressing down with the full weight required, the note did not speak and the result was plain to everyone listening. The modern pneumatic or electric action is infinitely easier to handle and requires only the lightest of touch; but I doubt whether it insists on precision in the same way as its predecessor.

Once again I had to embark on the hard chores of technical exercises. This time, in addition to the work on the keyboard, there was the introduction of the pedal board for the feet. There were exercises not only for the left hand alone and the right hand alone, but also for the feet, first separately and then together. Gradually I was working towards a stage where both hands, sometimes on separate manuals, would be co-ordinated with my feet on the pedals. Yet, somehow, practising in this way gave me rather more satisfaction than scales and arpeggios on the piano. What soon became abundantly clear to me was that the technique of playing an organ is in every respect different from that needed for the piano. On the piano, the light and shade, the strength and quality of the sound, depend entirely upon the touch, modified only by the sustaining and dampening pedals. On the organ, the touch itself cannot affect any of these qualities. The touch can provide the rhythm and precision but everything else is produced by the registration on each manual, the combination of stops used, the coupling of the manuals and the volume of the sound allowed by the opening or closing of the swell boxes.

Our parish organist had a leaning towards the French organ composers, particularly the more brilliant of them, such as Guilmant and Widor, but he started me off, after some simple pieces, with the short Bach preludes and fugues. Then I moved on to Bach's longer works and the Mendelssohn sonatas. Occasionally I had the opportunity of playing for services. Accompanying the psalms was always the trickiest part and leading the congregation in the hymns the most thrilling; it was, after all, the only occasion on which I could use full organ, though it was indicated to me at times that my choice of registration for both psalms and hymns was thought to be a little too vivid. Psalm 107 provides plenty of opportunity for this in its description of the storm and subsequent calm affecting 'They that go down to the sea in ships'. 'Does the organ at such times give you a sense of power?' I am often asked. 'Yes' is the answer. But not of power over people: it is the power of contributing sound to the general uplift of those making music together.

While I was learning the organ and conducting the mixed-voice choir I began to study the more theoretical aspects of music in harmony and counterpoint. I was able to do this under the senior music master, Mr G.C.L. Neville, at my grammar school, Chatham House, Ramsgate. Mr

Neville was also the organist at the parish church. I became fascinated at discovering the intellectual basis on which chords were built up, how a tune could be harmonized in various ways, how the same theme could be introduced at different intervals in contrapuntal music and how the structure of a piece could be traced, just as can the bones of a body without the flesh upon them, or the skeleton of a building without the bricks and mortar over it. I soon realized that if I was to follow this through I needed to know far more about the history of music and the people who wrote and performed it. I had never found it particularly easy to remember dates of wars and battles, but I discovered it was absorbing to trace the history of music, beginning with what is usually thought to be its earliest and simplest form, 'Sumer is icumen in', as a single line or as a canon with four voices following one another at intervals, through to the highly charged and concentrated forms of the twentieth century, particularly Stravinsky. The contrapuntal music of the Elizabethans, the harmonic pieces of the Stuarts, the varied dances, fugal works and choral music of Bach and Handel, the classical sonata form as it was developed from Haydn and Mozart to Beethoven and Schubert, the Romantics of the nineteenth century, including the great symphonists and the programme music of so many of these composers, the operas of Mozart, Rossini and Verdi, and the *leitmotif,* or 'theme' music, of Wagner and Strauss showed me the part musical form can play in the impact that a composition makes upon you.

But is it really necessary to know all this in order to enjoy listening to a piece of music? Not at all. No more than it is necessary to know how a building is erected or a picture is painted in order to enjoy looking at them. And if you are just beginning to listen to music, don't bother about trying to understand it. Sit back and let it flow over you. Let it

23

make its own impact on you. If it does have an effect upon you emotionally, or intellectually, you will become interested enough to want to find out more about it and in particular, perhaps, more about why and how it does have an effect upon you personally. Once you reach this stage, you will find it easy and natural to understand how a composer has put the work together, how he has created the effects and how, in the normal course of events, he has developed something that has a wholeness about it, a unity, out of the individual themes from which he started. If you know how a painter has been able to transfer the impression from his eye to the canvas, you will certainly find more to enjoy in his painting. If you appreciate how skilful an architect has been in securing the balanced proportions that his building displays, this will add another dimension to your appreciation of his work. If you can follow with the mind, as well as with the ear, the growth of a musical composition, your appreciation of it will increase with every performance. It was in just such a way that I was beginning to listen to orchestral pieces.

I had to do this very largely by means of the wireless, as radio was then called. As a young boy I had listened through earphones to a crystal set, but by now we possessed a wireless set with a loudspeaker. At that time the Isle of Thanet was not on the visiting list of the touring symphony orchestras and I had no opportunity of hearing a live orchestra playing symphonic music near my home. There was, of course, a school orchestra, which I often accompanied and sometimes conducted, but this was not as adventurous as the youth orchestras of today and never attempted to play major symphonic works. The BBC was steadily broadcasting its symphony concerts once a week for nine months of the year, and although it sometimes meant using them as background music while preparing for the inevitable school examinations, I was very often

able just to sit back and listen. When it came to August and September
the radio gave us the Promenade concerts in full measure. Every night,
wherever I was, I would try to get within reach of a loudspeaker to listen. But my real objective, of course, was to get to the concerts
themselves. I managed to do this for a few nights each season by staying
with friends in London who did not mind putting me up and then discovering that I disappeared every evening, very often first to queue and
then to stand for a good two hours in the auditorium of the Queen's
Hall, feasting on the packed programmes that Sir Henry Wood and his
orchestra used to produce.

It was at these Promenade concerts that I first learned most of my
orchestral music. The general arrangements then were much simpler
than now. One orchestra played throughout the eight weeks. It rehearsed
every morning and played every evening. As a result, it was sometimes
under-rehearsed, especially with a new work, and by the end of the season was showing signs of exhaustion, though the fervour of the last night
always restored the players' adrenalin and made up for some of the more
obvious weaknesses that had developed. The main difference, then from
now, was that the season was designed to cover all the major works of
the great composers from Bach to Elgar and to concentrate many of
them in evenings devoted to one composer or, at the most, two at a
time. This had the advantage that by listening to a number of works in
the same programme we could trace the development of the composer's
mind, and that by attending on a fixed night each week we could cover
most of a composer's orchestral repertoire. For me, Beethoven on Friday
was the great night, closely followed by Haydn, Mozart and sometimes
Bach, usually on Wednesdays. Tuesday tended to be a night for new or
lesser-known works. Sometimes it was used for English composers

alone. I found extracts from Wagner operas on Monday nights difficult to take. This didn't prevent me from making the attempt, but I realize now that I had little or no understanding of either the literary or the musical aspects of Wagner's art. Any impact that Monday night at the Proms did make on me came from the swelling mass of sound, rich and luxuriant, sweeping over me, and from the resonant voices of the singers soaring over the tumult. Somehow the stocky figure of Sir Henry Wood, with his characteristic wide-sweeping beat, the surging Wagnerian crescendos and the voices battling above them all seemed to be of a piece; but they still did not convert me to Wagner. Indeed, it was another twenty-five years before I began seriously to study him and his work and gradually to find enjoyment in it. Now where would I be, I wonder, without the splendour of *Die Meistersinger,* the intense passion of *Tristan* and the compulsive music drama of *The Ring?*

I soon discovered a way of persuading the authorities to allow me into the morning rehearsals of the Proms. A letter about my music at school and my intention of becoming a music student initially did the trick and got me a pass. Having once convinced them of this, I was able, by getting round the doorman and then standing at the back and keeping quiet, to slip in on other occasions, a habit that I have continued up to this day. Thus I was able to listen to Sir Henry Wood at work, to watch how he handled the orchestra and soloists and to see how he managed to get through so much in a single rehearsal. It was certainly a business-like, no-nonsense performance, and from it I learned a great deal, in particular how important it is to know when you go on to the rostrum precisely the time available to each particular item in the programme. It was there, too, that I first realized that it was not enough to know what you wanted; you also had to be able to indicate it clearly to some ninety to a hundred experienced and hardboiled musicians. From then on I never ceased to study the techniques of individual conductors: not content with listening to the finished product, I found it impossible not to watch and analyse at the same time how it was being created.

Sir Henry Wood conducted with a wide, steady beat, feet planted slightly astride and firmly on the rostrum, his body moving with the sound. Compared with some of the gymnastic or ballet-like performances we see today, his would probably be considered dull and rather routine. Yet there was a lesson in it for me. The first requirement of a conductor, especially if he is spending his time with amateur choirs and orchestras, is to be able to give a beat that no one can question. If it can be aesthetic at the same time, so much the better, but what really matters is that the group you are conducting should be held firmly together, no matter what happens, given the rhythmic drive essential for the work concerned and led to produce a body of sound that is not only precise but also beautiful.

The Proms today are, of course, in many ways very different from those I have been describing. The BBC performed a great public service when they undertook responsibility for them after Sir Henry Wood's death. It was fortunate that Sir Malcolm Sargent was there, with all his verve and flair, to continue the process of popularizing orchestral music. More recently there has been a wide variety of developments, including the presentation of complete operas from Glyndebourne after the season has finished, the inclusion of major choral works such as Bach's St Matthew Passion and Beethoven's Mass in D, and the introduction of a large number of new works, many specially commissioned for the Proms. The burden of the season is now shared among a considerable number of orchestras. This not only lightens the strain and improves the standard of performance, it also gives us the opportunity of hearing the leading provincial orchestras in their own specialities, as well as the other London orchestras besides those of the BBC. It is still the greatest strength of British musicians that their sight-reading is so exceptional, but I have no doubt at all that this new situation is to be preferred: the Proms, along with the Edinburgh Festival, are now an integral part of the international circuit for the great orchestras of the world on their summer tours. In 1996, for example, the Oslo, New York and Berlin Philharmonic Orchestras all gave two concerts within a ten-day period!

Although the Promenade concerts have been at the Albert Hall since the Queen's Hall was destroyed during the war, today many additional concerts are held in places such as Westminster Cathedral or the Roundhouse, either on Sundays or instead of the normal evening concert. Chamber music and singing by small choirs are now often included, and we have also witnessed late-night jazz concerts, sitar concerts and a wonderful performance of Negro spirituals. All this is to the good, but I sometimes wonder whether young people now get from the Proms as solid grounding in the basic works of European music as I and my generation did sixty years ago. If not, it is a pity, for there is no better way for the student to acquire this kind of grounding, and I myself shall always be grateful to the Promenade concerts for playing such a large part in my musical education. I still return when I see an evening or an item that attracts my interest. Now I sit in a box looking at that enthusiastic mass of young people, many perhaps hearing these works for the first time, and whose enthusiasm so dramatically and so obviously transmits itself to the performers. It always brings back many memories of the evenings I have enjoyed down there standing in the prom.

CHAPTER TWO

BALLIOL, BACH AND BROADSTAIRS

——

One evening, towards the end of my first term at Oxford, I found a note waiting for me on the table in my room. It read quite simply, 'Dear Heath, I am so glad to be able to let you know at once that we elected you tonight to the Organ Scholarship.' It was signed by the Dean, the Rev. M.R. Ridley. I had achieved my objective. From the following autumn I would be organ scholar at Balliol College, responsible for playing Evensong on Sundays and Morning Service at eight o'clock on weekdays. I would be directly involved in the Balliol concerts held in Hall on each alternate Sunday evening and I could play a more prominent part in the musical life of the university. It meant also that financially life would be somewhat easier. The scholarship – £80 a year – was not one of the most valuable offered by the college, and £80 does not seem a large amount now, but to me in those days it meant a great deal.

I had gone up to Balliol in October 1935 from grammar school as a commoner. For some time I had set my heart on getting to Oxford, and Balliol in particular. As with so many youthful decisions, it is a little difficult at this distance of time to rationalize this one, but having read everything I could get my hands on about Oxford I was attracted by Balliol's intellectual attainments and by the fact that wealth and privilege seemed to carry little weight there. Moreover, Oxford's long connection with those in politics and public life acted as a magnet for me. The fact that I did not succeed in getting an open scholarship in modern subjects meant that I could only take up entrance to the college that had accepted me with the help of a grant from a charitable foundation, a loan from the Kent Education Committee (to be repaid on the completion of my course) and funds from my parents, who had to struggle to make the money available. The Balliol organ scholarship enabled me to relieve them of most of the burden they had undertaken and at the same time allowed me to join college and university clubs and take part in their activities. Indeed, I had come up to Balliol knowing that the organ scholarship would become vacant in my first year and determined to do everything possible to keep myself at Oxford by winning it. The previous year I had tried for the organ scholarship at St Catherine's, Cambridge, admittedly rather half-heartedly, and at Keble College, Oxford, without success.

Keble was, in many ways, the Blue Riband of organ scholarships. It was true that Christ Church, New College and Magdalen all had senior organists and choirs of distinction, but Keble had produced many of the leading organists in the country and the Keble scholar was organist of the chapel in his own right. I went to Keble for the examination in some fear and trepidation, for I was young and inexperienced as well as having had insufficient tuition. On such occasions the set pieces are never the main problem, and I did not find the transposition from one key into another – so necessary for lowering the pitch of many of our hymns and chants so that they can be sung by an undergraduate congregation – too troublesome. I had also had to master the form of accompaniment for plainsong, something I enjoyed immensely, but when it came to improvisation on a theme produced by the examiner, I was at a loss. It was very soon clear to me that I was not going to become organ scholar at Keble. The examiner, kind and considerate, was Dr Thomas Armstrong, himself a former organ scholar of Keble and by then organist at Christ Church and conductor of the Oxford Bach Choir. This was my first meeting with the man who was later to become musical director of the Balliol concerts and whose son, Robert Armstrong, himself no mean musician, was to be my Principal Private Secretary at 10 Downing Street for nearly four years.

After my experiences at St Catherine's, Cambridge, and Keble, Oxford, I knew fairly exactly what would be required to get through the examination for an organ scholarship. As soon as I got to Oxford, I concentrated on extra tuition in preparation for the test in December. I took lessons twice a week from the organist at St Aldate's, and I was able to practise on the splendid three-manual modern instrument there. I also practised on the organ in Balliol because I knew all the competitors would be asked to play on it, and there was therefore some advantage in getting used to it, particularly as it was an old two-manual instrument with tracker action, stops that were heavy to pull out, and a straight pedal board, rather than the modern fan-shaped pedal board, all of which were hazards for the unsuspecting. When the day for the examination came, I concentrated on four pieces. The first was Bach's Prelude in E Flat, commonly called 'St Anne', based on the tune that is well known as that for the first line of the hymn 'O God our help in ages past'. The second was one of the trio sonatas of Bach. Simple as those may seem, with a single line of notes from each hand on a different manual and the feet on the pedal board, they are, as every organist knows, amongst the most difficult of works to play effectively. Thirdly, I chose

Mendelssohn's Sonata No. 2 in C Minor, a splendid work, which had always been a favourite of mine, as well as of the organist of St Peter's-in-Thanet, and, finally, a quiet piece by Vaughan Williams, based on the Welsh tune 'Rhosymedre'. In addition, I was well prepared to carry out the transposition of hymn tunes and chants and, if necessary, some improvisation.

The examiner was Dr Ernest Walker, one of Oxford's most interesting musical characters – slightly stooping, well bearded, with a high voice and piercing laugh. I had seen him at the Balliol concerts with his friends the two Deneke sisters. For many years he had been director of the concerts and never failed to appear at them. In chapel, he asked me to play the Mendelssohn Sonata, but stopped me before I could embark on the build-up of the fugue in the last movement, saying that he wanted to hear the Vaughan Williams. After that he listened to the whole of the Bach St Anne fugue. I did some transposition and that was that. He seemed pleased. I kept clear of everyone while the other competitors were playing. It was only when I got the note on my table the same evening that I knew of my success. I was glad they had decided so quickly.

After I had been elected organ scholar of Balliol I got to know Ernest Walker well. From time to time he would invite me to tea at his home in north Oxford, a typical Victorian house with heavy furniture and a rather gloomy interior. There he would discuss the college concerts and what was being performed at the Holywell Music Room, in which I was now taking a considerable interest. What I enjoyed most, however, was listening to his recollections of musicians and performances. He had known Brahms, and even possessed some of Brahms's original manuscripts, which he allowed me to see. He was, to me, a link between contemporary music and one of the great symphonists of all time.

It was through Ernest Walker that my interest in Brahms was first seriously aroused, and I soon concentrated my attention on his symphonies, beginning with the Fourth, his last. Its romantic opening, with drooping strings, followed by an upward answer, the simple horn tune of the second movement, and the vibrant Scherzo leading into the splendour of the last movement based on an oft-repeated theme, all still give me intense enjoyment. For the newcomer it is the last movement that is difficult to understand, but even without detailed knowledge of the structure one cannot help but be carried away as the mass of sound builds up to its climax. It is the crowning achievement of the work.

I got to know Brahms's First Symphony when Toscanini brought the BBC Symphony Orchestra to play in the New Theatre at Oxford. Toscanini had just begun to conduct again in England. It was said that he would only conduct the BBC Symphony Orchestra, but seldom outside London. For us in Oxford it was a remarkable event. The intensity of his performance of this symphony and his long wide beat remain vividly in my memory, together with the spaciousness of his treatment of this work. As Toscanini launched into the major theme of the last movement, warmly and vigorously, I felt deep emotion welling within me. He made me feel that everything that had come before had been a preparation for this – the mark of a totally satisfying performance.

Since then, I have come to love too the freshness and spontaneity of Brahm's Third Symphony; the glorious exuberance of its opening, the simplicity of the slow movement, the sad lilt of the third movement, and the forceful jollity of the leaping tune of the last. I wish it were played more often. The Second Symphony I have heard on innumerable occasions; it is the one that makes the least impact on me. Perhaps Brahms was drained after the immense effort involved in creating the First

Symphony. It seems to me to be lacking in depth.

It used to be fashionable to criticize Brahms because of his lack of orchestral colour. It is certainly true that he did not use his palette for the purpose of showing off orchestral technique, but there are few glories like that of a full orchestra playing the last movement of Brahms's First Symphony. As with all great composers, he was able to express the whole gamut of human emotion, but, above all, I found that he was able to write music which expressed the sheer joy of being alive. Nothing does this better than one of his early works, the Serenade in A. How often I have played the recording of that delightful piece made under Pablo Casals at the Marlboro Festival, set in the heart of the wooded hills of Vermont, while sitting at Chequers on a summer evening looking out on the peaceful English countryside.

I was once taken by surprise by the intimacy of music-making in public when I heard Myra Hess play Brahms's First Piano Concerto in D Minor with Dimitri Mitropoulos conducting the New York Philharmonic Orchestra in 1955 on one of its visits to the Festival Hall in London. The piano part of Brahms's First Concerto is fiendish, but it is not intended as a showpiece for the soloist's technique. It is only when the technical difficulties can be overcome and taken in their stride that pianists can begin to convey the depths of Brahms's music in the Concerto. It then appears extraordinarily simple. That night, in the Festival Hall, I suddenly realized that Myra Hess, Mitropoulos and the New York Philharmonic were just making music together; as an audience we might just as well not have been there. She was totally involved in the beauty of Brahms; he stood beside her in an ill-fitting tail coat and baggy trousers, his long arms by his side, hardly moving; the orchestra was at one with both of them. There was no attempt to show off; Brahms was

—

simply allowed to speak for himself through the piano and the orchestra. That was a night to remember.

—

The Deneke sisters, Margaret and Helena, close friends of Ernest Walker, were among those most active in Oxford musical life. Whenever I went to their house in Norham Gardens, in north Oxford, I knew that there would be musicians of interest to meet: either the great going to play in Lady Margaret Hall, where Helena was a Fellow, or yet another young prodigy – pianist, violinist or cellist – whom Margaret was helping to get established. Of the great, the one I most wanted to meet was Sir Donald Tovey. He had been the first composition scholar at Balliol and had become for us a legend in his own lifetime. His work as conductor of the Reid Orchestra in Edinburgh was widely admired, but his compositions, some of which the critics found 'too eclectic', with their obvious debt to the Romantics, were less appreciated. It was believed that if he had chosen he could have been the greatest pianist of his time, and his writings on music, though now somewhat dated, were the touchstone for my generation. One Sunday afternoon, when I went to the Denekes for tea, I found Tovey there; alas, his hands were badly crippled from arthritis. Nevertheless, he sat and played for us. Despite his infirmity, his deep understanding of the music came through to us in that small group sitting around the drawing room. He produced a beautiful tone; he made the piano sing in a way that was remarkable. He refused to play on anything except a Bösendorfer, a piano noted for its soft tonal quality. I can still picture him sitting quietly on that piano stool, a large, burly figure with a craggy head, producing that lovely tone. How I wish I had heard him in his prime.

Tovey died twenty years before Bruckner's and Mahler's great rise to popularity in Europe and America during the fifties and sixties, although, as we shall see, he partly foresaw it. At Oxford, we had just begun to discover the delights of Bruckner and the excitement of Mahler. It was Bruckner's Fourth Symphony that I stumbled upon first, on a recording that I played constantly. It had a freshness and spontaneity about it – perhaps now I would say a little naivety – which conveyed to me the real joy of music-making. Of course it is a long work but I have never quibbled at that in music. For us in the thirties, threatened as we were by dictatorship and war, Bruckner seemed to bring something reassuring from the world of nature into our lives. In many ways Bruckner's Fourth appeared to be a continuation of Schubert's great C Major Symphony. Later, after the war, I pursued the rest of Bruckner's works, until I experienced the strength and splendour of the Seventh and Eighth symphonies. If Bruckner's Fourth is still the most popular of his symphonies, without doubt the Seventh and Eighth are the greatest. The Adagio in the Seventh builds up into the most powerful and emotional movement in his music. Bruckner considered his finest work to be the *Te Deum,* and it is significant that at the culmination of this personal expression of faith, to the words *'Non confundar in aeternum',* he reintroduces the theme of the Adagio of the Seventh Symphony.

I got to know Mahler through *Das Lied von der Erde,* never more beautifully sung than by Kathleen Ferrier. Compared with Bruckner this was strange music indeed, but it had its own fascination. Nature is strongly present in Mahler, too, but here it is felt as a hideous torment contrasting with spiky cheerfulness. In the sixties I became preoccupied with Mahler's symphonies; each is part of the development of a sustained philosophy, yet each varies greatly in its structure, material and final impact. The best advice I can give to the listener unfamiliar with Mahler is to

follow the composer's own progression from the First Symphony
onwards. Every conductor today seems to have a different idea of what
Mahler wanted, but I know of nothing better than the few existing
recordings by Bruno Walter (now happily restored to the catalogue),
who himself worked with Mahler and knew his mind.

In his essay on Mahler's Fourth Symphony, written in the thirties,
Tovey showed a perception of both Bruckner and Mahler, combined with
an acute understanding of British musical approach and taste, which I
find quite astonishing for the time at which it was written. In the midst
of a brilliant piece he says: 'We do not wish it generally known, but we
would all like to write like Mahler if we dared; and we all think that we
could. The martyr whom he most nearly resembles is Bruckner but
Mahler is anything but helpless and raises none of the sympathy of a
naive artist struggling for self expression. Far from it. We find his facility deadly.' Later he sums up his views by writing: 'The musical culture
of Great Britain will probably be the better for the rise of a vogue for
Bruckner and Mahler; and Mahler will do so much more than Bruckner,
because his mastery will discourage the cult of amateurish things which
keeps us contented with ignorance and ready to believe that ineptitude
is noble in itself; and the good taste which is ready to take offence at
Mahler's sentimentality will be all the better for being shocked.' What
foresight, what an understanding of the British musical sensibility at that
time, what wise advice. What Tovey foresaw has come to pass, and I have
no doubt that our musical culture is all the better for it.

There was little chance of hearing performances of either Bruckner
or Mahler during my time at Oxford. Their works appeared seldom at
the Proms. No doubt the scale of the forces required for Mahler in particular, especially for his Eighth Symphony, the 'Symphony of a

Thousand', accounted in some measure for this, and the inadequacy of rehearsal time compounded the difficulties. This has now changed completely; hardly a season goes by without, at the very least, a 'Resurrection' and a Bruckner Eighth! One early example, however, was the Prom in 1963, when I heard Stokowski – he was already over eighty – conducting the London Symphony Orchestra in Mahler's 'Resurrection' Symphony. It was a superb performance in the Stokowski manner, rich, warm and vibrant. At the end the crowded promenade went wild with excitement. To their delight, Stokowski returned and, after a performance that would have exhausted almost any other conductor, picked up his baton and played the second half of the last movement again. On only one other occasion have I ever heard part of a work played again as an encore. That was when Giulini conducted the New Philharmonia Choir and Orchestra in the Verdi Requiem at Parma in 1963 for the celebration of the 150th anniversary of Verdi's birth. After a scintillating performance of the Sanctus, the excited audience refused to allow the work to proceed. Giulini had no alternative but to repeat the Sanctus. To the British, such an explosion of spontaneous feeling in the middle of a Requiem Mass, and followed at that by a repetition of the Sanctus, would have been completely incomprehensible; but to the Italians it was a perfectly natural outpouring of their joy and delight, not only in a magical piece of musical writing but also in a meticulous yet inspiring performance of it.

The orchestras visiting Oxford did not bring Bruckner and Mahler with them. If anything it was Sibelius whose virtues were proclaimed, whose works were more and more widely performed. His Second Symphony, much akin to its Romantic predecessors, with its wide, sweeping tunes and orthodox orchestration, was already popular. In the

Town Hall at Oxford I heard his Fifth Symphony, whose electrifying climax had everyone on their feet at the end cheering. Sir Thomas Beecham brought the Royal Philharmonic Orchestra to play Sibelius's Seventh Symphony, all in one movement, a great favourite of his, at the Sheldonian Theatre. That was more difficult to understand at first hearing, but with repetition it became clear how Sibelius's mind was moving. After a period of being relatively unfashionable, the works of Sibelius are now popular again – thanks, in no small part, to the brilliant advocacy of Sir Colin Davis and the LSO.

It was not until I got to Boston on a debating tour of the United States in December 1939 that I heard Mahler in the flesh, so to speak. There, in that resonant Symphony Hall, the home of the Boston Symphony Orchestra, I heard Koussevitzky conduct the Adagio from Mahler's Ninth Symphony. It was an intensely moving experience to hear Koussevitzky, now primarily remembered as Leonard Bernstein's great mentor, draw such a depth of tone from the strings and to listen to the mild-toned brass blending in so warmly. Yet, looking back, I find myself asking how one of the world's greatest conductors, with a superb orchestral instrument at his command, could have extracted just one movement from a Mahler symphony for performance in a concert programme? Would he have done it with the Adagio of Beethoven's Ninth? Or of Brahms's Second? Or of Elgar's First? I do not think so. Even in 1939, there was still something strange about the way Mahler was treated.

—

As soon as I had settled in at Balliol, I applied to join the Oxford Bach Choir. After an audition, which was very largely a question of sight-reading and deciding which sort of voice I had got, I was accepted as a first bass. The choir met for rehearsal every Monday in the lecture theatre at the University Museum, a big room with seats steeply raked to the back. The conductor stood where the lecturer would normally have been and just in front of him was a piano with the accompanist. I soon found that it was not just a case of being a member of the choir; there was a marked tendency to form smaller groups within the choir as a whole. Perhaps the Balliol group was particularly clannish in this; at any rate we always made a point of sitting together on the topmost bench, the basses on the right facing the conductor and the tenors on the left. The sopranos and altos, from the women's colleges and from the city and its surrounding villages, were on either side of us. One thing that contributed to the Balliol men remaining together as a group was that we were invited each Sunday morning to the house of one of our Senior Fellows, Cyril Bailey, a most distinguished Latin scholar and writer, to practise the bass and tenor parts on our own. At these private mini-rehearsals I was expected both to sing and to accompany at the same time.

In my first term we were rehearsing Vaughan Williams's 'Sea' Symphony, a work with which the Oxford Bach Choir felt it had a particular connection. Although the first performance at Leeds had not been a conspicuous success, the second, at Oxford, was a triumph. Vaughan Williams is said to have written later in Sir Hugh Allen's score: 'I thought I had written an unsingable work but tonight you have sung it magnificently.' For me it is one of Vaughan Williams's most effective compositions. It thrilled me from the beginning. Its exciting opening, a short vigorous trumpet declaration, followed by the sudden, dramatic entry of the choir, 'Behold the sea itself ...', sounds as the choir resolves the opening chords like a great wave just on the point of breaking. It rolls over and then comes the swell of the rollers 'and on its limitless, heaving breast, the ships'. The slow movement conveys that feeling of limitless space and time one knows so well at sea, that feeling of unity in the world. The Scherzo, the dancing waves shimmering and twinkling in the sun, is a far from easy movement for a big choir to carry out with precision and the necessary lightness of tone. Diction, too, is a problem, at the speed required here. In contrast, the last movement brings peace: there are some who feel that Vaughan Williams develops it at too great a length but so heavenly is its last theme, particularly when sung by the soprano and baritone soloists, 'O! We can wait no longer, we too take ship, O soul', that I find it entirely acceptable. Walt Whitman's words, used by Vaughan Williams, are amongst the most moving he ever wrote. For me, the 'Sea' Symphony was not some passing phenomenon: I have come to love it more and more as the years have gone by. It comes constantly into my mind when I sail and I realize how well Vaughan Williams was able to express the feel of the sea. When, after a day's racing on the Solent, *Morning Cloud* is one of an apparently endless series of boats of every size, shape and kind, all returning from their pleasure to their moorings, Whitman's words 'a motley procession with many a fleck of foam' seem particularly appropriate to us all.

The Bach Choir's plans to sing the 'Sea' Symphony early in 1936 were interrupted by the sudden death of King George V in January that year. When we got back for the beginning of term we found that it had been decided that the choir should sing the *German Requiem* by Brahms in the Sheldonian Theatre as a memorial to the late King. We had just ten days in which to rehearse this work. The older members of the choir of course already knew it well, but for the great majority of us it was the first time we had ever sung it. Sir Hugh Allen, the Heather Professor of Music at Oxford at that time, was returning to conduct us. He was the doyen of Oxford musicians and had established a national reputation for his performance of this work.

Sir Hugh was well known to my generation of students by repute as a remarkable though somewhat fearsome man. After becoming a church organist at the age of eleven in his home town of Reading, he was appointed assistant organist at Chichester Cathedral. There he indulged his love of the sea, which remained with him all his life, and bought his first boat. He went on to be organ scholar at Christ's College, Cambridge. It is said that when he first arrived at the college he told the cab to wait, saying to the porter at the lodge: 'Don't move my bags. I want to look around to see if I like this place first.' He then went straight on to be organist at St Asaph Cathedral in Wales, then at Ely Cathedral, and later became organist at New College, Oxford. For many years he was both Director of the Royal College of Music in London and Professor of Music in Oxford. For more than a quarter of a century he was conductor of the Oxford Bach Choir. During this time he not only built up the choir into a sound musical instrument, but also established a reputation for wit, although with a somewhat caustic tongue. We looked forward eagerly to his appearance at the first rehearsal. He immediately took a grip on the situation and drove us relentlessly. As we had so few rehearsals he kept us much later than usual at night, so much so that on one occasion some of the ladies tried to slip out quietly and unobtrusively down the side of the lecture hall to catch their last bus home. Suddenly spotting this, Sir Hugh stopped everything, threw his baton to the floor, put his hands on his hips and glared at the unfortunate women as now, with all eyes upon them, they stumbled far from silently down the steps. Then, looking up at Cyril Bailey, probably the senior member of the choir and sitting among the basses, he exploded:

'Good God, Cyril, they are the same women creeping out now who crept out fifty years ago!' It was after some such similar occasion that Sir Hugh, walking to the Music School in the Clarendon Building, found himself confronted by an irate lady who stopped him in his tracks and said, very forcefully: 'Sir Hugh, you must not go on being so rude to the altos', to which Sir Hugh replied without pausing: 'Madam, those whom the Lord loveth, them also he chasteneth', and passed on.

The final rehearsal for the Requiem was held on the Sunday morning of the performance. The Balliol contingent, with its usual farsightedness, had decided to occupy the front row in the Sheldonian because it appeared to be the only place where the wooden benches were covered with cushions. We soon learned our mistake; Sir Hugh tapped his baton and said: 'You can put away all those copies, you must know it by heart now.' The rest of the choir discreetly lowered their copies behind other people's backs. We had to put ours down in front of us and manage with surreptitious glances from time to time.

It was the second movement that gave him the greatest difficulty. The timpanist could not meet Sir Hugh's exacting demands for a relentless dotted rhythm in 'All flesh doth perish as the grass'. 'One last go,' said Sir Hugh ominously, 'and just watch me.' He started again and then, with eyes fixed purposefully on the face of the timpanist, he marched menacingly through the orchestra, step by step, beat by beat, towards this wretched creature now cowering lower and lower over his kettledrums. We, too, watched petrified as Sir Hugh, now hammering the dotted beat with his fist into the hollow of his hand, finally achieved the result he wanted. Never, before or since, even as Government Chief Whip, have I seen intimidation used to such good effect!

Sir Hugh's conception of the German Requiem had spaciousness and dignity, delicacy and at the same time intensity; it was never rushed or forced, but had all the assurance and balance that stems from a deep understanding of the work. From the quiet, perfectly sustained chords of the opening, 'Blest are they that mourn', the rhythmic intensity of 'All flesh doth perish as the grass', the fervent build-up to 'Death where is thy sting?' – surely one of the most splendid harmonic progressions in choral music – and the two great fugues, interspersed with the soaring soprano solo, 'Ye who now sorrow', through to the final chords of the Requiem as they die away, all this he knit into one imposing structure. The impact on me that Sunday afternoon was lasting. From the many performances I have heard since I have learned, rather sadly, one thing. I have never gained as much satisfaction from hearing the German Requiem or playing recordings of it as I did from that one occasion on which I rehearsed and sang it. In fact this feeling applies not only to the Brahms, but to almost every work in which I have sung. It may be that the mere physical act of singing provides an outlet for the emotional content of the work, which cannot be obtained by sitting in a concert hall or room and listening to it. It may also be that, having identified oneself closely with a work as a result of singing it, the difficulty of appreciating other performances becomes that much greater.

I sang two other major works with the Bach Choir whilst I was at Oxford, Haydn's *The Seasons* and Beethoven's *Missa Solemnis. The Seasons* is an enchanting work, too little performed in Britain. Haydn maintains the classical form both in the solo arias and in the choruses, which have a strength and beauty of their own; but what makes the work so delightful, both to listen to and to sing, is the way the orchestral accompaniment illustrates and illuminates the text in musical terms. Of course, no orchestral instrument can give a perfect imitation of a bird flying or a dog sniffing around, though some electronic instruments and in the old days the Wurlitzer cinema organs have attempted to do so. What instruments can do is give an indication in recognizable musical language of what is going on. Haydn's language in this respect is very simple, as is Beethoven's in the 'Pastoral' Symphony.

When we come to Beethoven's Mass in D we are dealing with a very different sort of work. Here Beethoven was struggling to express the depths of emotion that lay within him. The struggle is all too obvious in large stretches of the work, a struggle that reflects itself in the difficulties which face any choir singing it. It requires, I believe, a relentless drive to stand any chance of re-creating Beethoven's efforts to reach the sublime. The effect cannot ever be achieved by a choir which is itself struggling. Paradoxically, the choir needs to be able to produce even more than Beethoven demanded; it is only then, with an intense impetus from the conductor, that the work can make its impact. Even when Beethoven grants us a brief respite, such as in the lovely Benedictus with the solo violin obbligato, the work must always be moving forward right up to its last passionate demand for peace, 'Dona nobis pacem'. Some think that the work has a good many rough edges; in my view it is quite wrong to smooth them out. This was at the heart of a discussion I had with Giulini one day at the Edinburgh Festival and again later when he came to 10 Downing Street, while he was preparing for a performance of the Mass in St Paul's Cathedral. His is a beautifully controlled performance in which the quality of the soloists, choir and orchestra is always happily balanced, but for me it is not Beethoven. In the process, the rough edges have been smoothed out. For me the Mass epitomizes man's struggle through life and at the end it is a *demand* for peace, not peace itself, that remains.

In addition to the Haydn and Beethoven we also learned two smaller Bach works, 'Sing to the Lord a new song' and 'Jesu, priceless treasure', which we sang in the chapel of St George's, Windsor, a new experience from the point of view of acoustics. As an organ scholar, I was taken up into the organ loft by the chapel organist, W.H. — later Sir William — Harris, so that I could see the double console there. The two consoles were identical and placed at right-angles to each other to form an L. This enabled duets to be played on the organ, though there are remarkably few works, to my knowledge, written in this form. One console could, of course, have been used to provide the orchestral accompaniment for the other when works such as Handel's organ concerti were being played. Although obviously great fun for organists who might want to do this or to improvise an echo piece in which each answered the other, it was a somewhat extravagant arrangement. When the organ at St George's was afterwards rebuilt, one console was removed and the organ assumed the normal form. I have not seen any other organ in the world that had two consoles arranged in this way. There are, of course, many instances in churches and cathedrals where the main console is near the organ and where there is a replica of it in the nave, so that the organist can be close to the choir and congregation on some festive occasion. There are a number of cathedrals where, in addition to the main organ, there is a small chamber or pipe organ available in another part of the cathedral to accompany the choir. In the chapel of the Escorial, the former palace of the kings of Spain outside Madrid, I found three organs, each of equal importance — one at the west end, one at the north and one at the south. I played the one at the south side, a magnificent baroque instrument, but I must confess I found it difficult to see how the three could be used together.

Until I went up to Oxford I had had little opportunity of hearing any chamber music. What a horrible phrase that is. Mention it on radio or television and the switch will immediately be turned to another channel. The mere sight of the words on a programme is enough to make anyone run a mile, resolving to have nothing whatever to do with this strange art, which conjures up in the mind pictures of scraping fiddles and cellos in quartets, or of sopranos warbling at interminable length without an apparent tune – and what is more, in other people's languages – or, perhaps worst of all, of over-stretched tenors failing to cope adequately with the thrashing chords of an overweening accompanist. Yet all 'chamber music' means is music to be played in the home or in the music room of a large house. Some of the most personal music ever written was composed for a trio, often a violin, a cello and a piano, or a string trio of violin, cello and viola, occasionally for three wind instruments or for individual combinations of instruments that composers fancied. Very often the pieces were written for particular artists, or groups of friends, and usually the composer played one of the instruments himself. The songs of Schubert, Schumann and Brahms, and in our own day Benjamin Britten, are among the most effective expressions of musical ideas, and as such they frequently depict the most intimate of human emotions – joy and sorrow, love, despair and death. Some contemporary music in this field may be difficult to comprehend, though not necessarily any more so than other music of our time, but the chamber works of Haydn and Mozart, Beethoven and Schubert, Schumann and Brahms for the most part make an immediate appeal. This is particularly true of the string quartets of Haydn and Mozart. For those who are thinking of exploring this kind of music, Beethoven's early quartets are attractive but they develop structurally and harmonically until his last quartets, amongst the finest ever written, become difficult to appreciate fully without sustained thought and repeated listening. At the end of his novel *Point Counter Point* Aldous Huxley leaves his principal character to die after putting on a record of the slow movement of Beethoven's penultimate quartet. It is true that this work has a quality of finality that only Beethoven achieved. I often wonder, however, whether Huxley's man would not have more peacefully left this earth if the record had been playing the final pages of Beethoven's last piano sonata in C minor.

It was at the Balliol Sunday evening concerts that I learned most of my chamber music. These concerts, held on every alternate Sunday evening during term in the college hall, had been started in 1885. Benjamin Jowett was the first Master of Balliol to encourage an interest in music in the college. He brought John Farmer from Harrow to be Director of Music at Balliol. John Farmer was very largely responsible for the compilation of the book of Harrow Songs, many of which he composed himself. Later, he put together a similar book of Balliol Songs.

John Farmer started the Musical Society at Balliol. The first programmes, rather like the first Promenade concerts, contained a considerable number of small individual items of a mixed variety. Gradually they moved towards their present format of a trio or quartet, normally playing two or three pieces, or a singer with piano accompanist in three or four groups of songs. One concert a term was set aside for a performance by members of the university. Most of the concerts were packed. The atmosphere was informal, with only the first third of the hall occupied by rows of chairs; in the remaining space people sat on tables and benches or anything else that was available, sometimes having to make do with the floor. These concerts had one tradition that no other college maintained. At the end of the concert, when the applause to the final item was dying, the Master, sitting in his corner chair in the front row, waved his programme aloft. The whole audience rose, faced the organ at the back of the hall and sang the chorale printed on the programme sheet. It gave the concert a tremendous finale. The organ at that time was hand-pumped and when the hall was full, the chorale long and splendid, it was a very exhausted and sweat-bedevilled 'scout', or college servant, who emerged from the side of the organ as we all disappeared into the night. When I go to a Balliol concert now, I automatically turn round at the end, expecting to hear the chorale tune blazing forth; but the tradition has lapsed, and we just shuffle out like any other audience anywhere else.

—

When I became organ scholar, I also became Secretary of the Musical Society. In addition to becoming involved in the planning of the programmes, I had the task of looking after the artists. Although a few were temperamental, most relished the prospect of playing to a large, attentive and enthusiastic student body. They knew that there would be nothing blasé about this audience, whose critical faculties were well honed. There were no separate facilities for artists, and they found themselves in one of the Senior Common Rooms before being led up a narrow iron staircase, to appear suddenly in the full blaze of lights in Hall.

The only time I was really taken aback during this time was when I was asked to look after the Busch Quartet at the Denekes' house in Norham Gardens, before they played a concert at Lady Margaret Hall. The Quartet, led by the great violinist Adolph Busch, was one of the most distinguished of the century, and they had been allotted time to rest between lunch and their performance at three o'clock. When I got them to their room, they immediately removed their jackets and ties, lay on the floor and proceeded to perform a variety of back-breaking exercises, which I was convinced would land them in the Radcliffe Infirmary traction department before they made it to Lady Margaret Hall. After this routine, however, they appeared totally relaxed and went on to produce a superb performance of a programme including the Verdi Quartet, an early work of his that is virtually his only surviving non-vocal piece, and a vigorous and tuneful composition, which would repay being reintroduced into our programmes.

At the Balliol concerts I heard for the first time many of the major works for trios, quartets and quintets, as well as cycles for the voice. Contemporary works were few and far between; the nearest thing was probably Ravel's Piano Trio. The lack of contemporary music in public performance was partially made up for by the private concerts which the Master, A.D. Lindsay, and Mrs Lindsay hosted in their own lodgings. It was there that I first heard Peter Pears singing the songs of Benjamin Britten, with the composer at the piano. The main purpose of the Balliol concerts, however, was similar to that of the Promenade concerts at this time: to provide a predominantly young audience with a solid grounding in the established classics, played and sung as well as possible.

Many works I first heard then still delight my memory, such as Beethoven's 'Archduke' Trio, surely one of the loveliest ever written. How many times since have I returned home late at night exhausted after a tiring day at the House of Commons; how many times did I go up to my flat at 10 Downing Street, after a tempestuous day of meetings of every kind, and put on a recording of the 'Archduke'? Its very first bars bring a calmness and repose that restore tranquillity to the troubled mind. Beethoven's first 'Razumovsky' Quartet, which I also first heard at Balliol, I find robust and intellectually stimulating, with its glorious melody in the first movement bracing one for sterner things to come, while Schubert's B Flat Trio is still sheer joy, bubbling Champagne, flowing along and carrying one with it whatever the difficulties of the day may be. Twice in Hall I heard the complete song cycle *Dichterliebe* by Schumann – both unforgettable occasions. There were frequently individual songs by the Lieder composers, but the *Dichterliebe* has always had a special place in my heart.

The concert performance at Balliol that I shall remember above all was given by Jelly d'Aranyi and Adila Fachiri accompanied on the piano by Sydney Watson in a superb rendering of Bach's Concerto for Two Violins in D Minor. The two sisters were already renowned for their performance of this piece, and never before or since, not even with the Oistrakhs, father and son, have I heard the slow movement, one violin answering another, so beautifully phrased and sustained. One did not miss the orchestral accompaniment. At the end there was a happy scene as, with all tension released, both sisters simultaneously threw their arms round Sydney Watson's neck and uninhibitedly kissed him.

This was an occasion with a special meaning for Balliol, for Ernest Walker had once brought Joachim, the greatest violinist of his day and a friend of Brahms, to Balliol to play at the concerts in Hall, and Joachim in his turn had brought the sisters, actually his great-nieces, to Balliol to give their first performances in England as girl prodigies. It was at the college concerts that they had made their reputation nearly thirty years before, and now they had returned to play for the next generation. It was a wonderfully moving experience of continuity in our music-making.

My main contribution to the concerts was to create the Balliol Choir, to which tenors and basses came from the college with a handful from Trinity, next door, and the sopranos and altos came from Somerville and Lady Margaret Hall with reinforcements from the other women's colleges. Our big opportunity came when we had the Thousandth Concert in 1937. Everyone taking part had to have some connection with Balliol. We sang Handel's coronation anthem, 'Zadok the Priest', and then the 'Songs from England's Helicon' by Ernest Walker, who paced up and down the back of the hall during rehearsals. These little-known pieces can be sung by a quartet or octet or by a full choir. They combine a sensibility and vigour, harmonic elegance and balanced structure, which make them perfect examples of this miniature art form. The harmonic progressions are tricky and they are not easy to sing well. The accompaniment requires a good pianist; maybe it is even better played on two pianos. We were fortunate in having George Malcolm at the piano, the composition scholar at Balliol at the same time as I was organ scholar. He had a brilliant technique and a fabulous memory for music. To him everything seemed to come easily and I envied him his facility.

Ernest Walker and Victor Hely-Hutchinson, a former composition scholar at the college and Professor of Music at Birmingham, now remembered for his pastiche of Handel in his setting of 'Old Mother Hubbard', played Bach's C Major Concerto for Two Pianos. Ernest Walker had the strange characteristic of always playing his left hand slightly before the right – so unusual was this that, it was said irreverently and probably apocryphally, it was recorded in the medical textbooks – the result being that the concerto became something of a scramble as his right hand tried to keep up with his left and Victor Hely-Hutchinson tried to keep up with both; it was certainly an exciting performance. William Harris and Sydney Watson played Donald Tovey's

'Balliol Dances' for four hands on one piano, reminiscent of the well-known waltzes by Brahms. In order to carry out the undertaking about college connections, Cyril Bailey announced in a charming speech at the end of the concert that 'both Bach and Handel had been made Honorary Fellows for the evening'.

Later, in the fifties and sixties, I was able to repay some of the debt I owed to the Balliol concerts by persuading others to play there. Yehudi and Hephzibah Menuhin played together three Beethoven sonatas, concluding with the 'Kreutzer'. They had a rapturous reception, which seemed to stun even them. Claudio Arrau played a monumental programme of Liszt. This time it was the audience who seemed to be taken aback. Only then did I realize that fresh generations of Oxford men had become accustomed to a delicate and – as I would describe it – anaemic kind of performance, the sort of playing that Smeterlin produced for my generation in the Mozart G Major Sonata. To hear Liszt played in a massive, scintillating way was to those students a revelation of how a great pianist can make the piano sound. It took me back to the concert that Rachmaninov had played at the New Theatre at Oxford in 1938. He, too, was one of the great masters of the piano. He included in his programme four of Chopin's Studies; the last, in which he swept up and down the keyboard with fingers apparently of steel, absolutely accurate and brilliantly under control, remains my most vivid memory of that concert. Of course the famous Rachmaninov Prelude in C Sharp Minor was produced as an encore and played without sentimentality: not for him, the composer, the folklore about the piece depicting the Kremlin bells sounding. For him it was one of his preludes, perfectly shaped, properly balanced, never to played perfunctorily or romantically, but another miniature to be meticulously executed.

Another aspect of music with which I became involved was providing music for plays, in particular for the Balliol Players and the Oxford University Dramatic Society, OUDS. The Balliol Players were a group who went on tour with a Greek play at the end of the summer term. It was very pleasant, after a strenuous academic year, to spend ten days moving through Oxfordshire, Berkshire, down to the West Country and then back to London, putting on the play once or twice a day. It was almost always performed in the open air, so to a certain extent we were at the mercy of the weather. When I was asked to write the music for Aristophanes' *The Acharnians,* I was helped by Walt Rostow, later to become Foreign Affairs Adviser at the White House to President Johnson. At the end of the spring term of 1939 I also did some arrangements for the OUDS production of *The Taming of the Shrew.*

By this time I was President of the Oxford Union Debating Society, for politics was my other love at the university, together with music. In arranging a programme of debates at the Union, I sought Sir Hugh Allen's help to persuade Sir Thomas Beecham to come down for the main debate of the term, the Presidential Debate. With his help everything was arranged. Sir Thomas, who was already well known, if not notorious, for his short, witty, often biting, off-the-cuff utterances in the middle and at the end of concerts, agreed to speak in the Union on the motion that 'This house would like to appoint a dictator' – with himself in mind. Alas! On the day on which he was due to come down to Oxford, I got a telegram saying that he was unable to appear – a feature of his activities that was becoming all too characteristic at that time. I fear that he lost his nerve. The same thing happened a fortnight later with Charles Laughton, who at the last moment could not bring himself to propose that 'This house prefers the poet to the pub.'

In the glorious summer of 1939 most of us at Oxford knew that a war was coming, but we did not allow the threat to spoil that summer. In fact, in some ways it made it more intensely enjoyable. One Sunday morning in May I drove up to London with Madron Seligman, a descendant of the American composer Edward MacDowell, and two girls. In the glorious sunshine we picnicked by the side of the road and then went on to Queen's Hall. There Toscanini conducted the BBC Orchestra and Choir in the Beethoven *Missa Solemnis*. It was a magnificent performance, hard, driving and precise but with a lovely tenderness in the Benedictus before the return to the anguished *'Dona nobis pacem'*. At the end there was utter silence. Inside the hall the choir called for peace. In the world outside they were preparing for war.

—

Both Christmas and Easter are still closely identified with music, even in an age that associates them less and less with religion. Easter-time performances of the Bach Passions still play to full houses, and Christmas carols are still sung with vigour across the Western world. For most of my life, I have conducted at least one carol concert every Christmas – in my home town of Broadstairs, in my constituency of Bexley or even, fleetingly, on the concourse of Waterloo Station! I first discovered the tradition of the town carol concert when I was at Oxford.

Every year, on the Sunday before Christmas, every citizen who could possibly do so packed into the town hall, headed by the mayor, aldermen and councillors. There they found a section of the Bach Choir, together with the Oxford Orchestra, consisting mostly of local residents, under the baton of Sir Hugh Allen. The object was for town and gown to join together at Christmastide to sing carols; the Christmas section of Handel's *Messiah* and part of Bach's *Christmas Oratorio* were also performed. But Sir Hugh Allen wanted more than that. He wanted the carols to be well sung, to be chosen from a much wider range than those heard on the doorstep, and the audience had to take part in the singing. But even that was not enough. He wanted the audience to learn new carols, and for this purpose the programme contained not only the words but also the melodic line of those carols he proposed to teach them. And, rather daringly, so the story had it, he would from time to time ask the mayor, councillors and aldermen to rise and sing a verse on their own. From everything I heard I could tell that this town carol concert was a considerable success and greatly valued by Oxford people. I was very much attracted by the idea and resolved that I would go home and do likewise.

When the following autumn came, in 1936, I wrote to the chairman of the Broadstairs and St Peter's Urban District Council, representing a population one-tenth that of the city of Oxford, setting out my proposal and asking if he and his colleagues would sponsor a town carol concert. Carefully omitting any suggestion that he and his fellow councillors might be required to sing a verse on their own, I emphasized that an act of this kind by the community would only be meaningful if it were done under his auspices. In due course I received a letter from the town clerk welcoming the idea and saying that the chairman of the council would not only allow me to describe this as a town carol concert under the council's sponsorship, but would also give it their personal support by appearing at the concert itself on the Sunday before Christmas. As a young undergraduate I had virtually taken all this for granted, but in retrospect I think it was a rather more daring project for me to have undertaken than it was for Sir Hugh Allen, a Professor of Music in the university.

Having embarked on the concert, I realized that it would require a good deal of organization. On the musical side I drew unashamedly on Oxford's experience; for the rest I managed to persuade the officers in the town council to co-operate by providing many of the facilities required. Fortunately, I also had an instrument to hand to take the place of the Oxford Bach Choir and Orchestra. This was 'Our Carol Party', together with an orchestra composed of local musicians who played together for their own enjoyment under the leadership of the sister of one of my school friends.

Our Carol Party had been formed in 1923, partly with the same aim as Sir Hugh's Oxford carollers, namely to show what carols were like when they were well sung. At the same time Our Carol Party wanted to raise money to provide a better Christmas for those in need. In 1926 I was invited to join this party of men and women, no doubt because as a chorister I could usefully fill in the treble solos, particularly the page in 'Good King Wenceslas'.

Joining Our Carol Party opened up a new vista for me, in terms of both carols and carollers. Here were carols we had never heard of, let alone sung in a Christmas carol service, at St Peter's-in-Thanet; some were French, some were German, some were English collected from the countryside, others were harmonizations of tunes already known to me. What was most striking was the precision, the rhythm and the polish with which they were sung. What is more, they were all unaccompanied, even when we were invited to sing indoors. The Party would never dream of allowing itself to be accompanied on a piano or any other instrument. All this made the singing much more interesting.

As for the carollers, from them I learned two things. First, that when we were singing we concentrated entirely on the quality of our sound. No matter how bitterly the winds blew on the North Foreland, or the snow drifted down around our ears, it was the standard of the performance that mattered. No matter how warm the hospitality inside someone's home, we must never allow ourselves to be distracted from the self-imposed task of producing a beautiful performance. But, and this was the second point, between the music we could, and did, thoroughly enjoy ourselves.

After the council had endorsed my proposal for a town carol service I set about enlarging the Carol Party to provide the choir for this event. As a result of approaching all the other choirs in the town, we augmented the Party to sixty people. Then we began rehearsals, not only in the carols but in the other items required for the concert. At the same time we had the task of getting parts for the orchestra, which agreed to play for us. The only hall available was one used for a concert party in the summer; the hall went under the romantic and somewhat unsuitable name of 'Bohemia'. It seated around 1,000 people, but it was far from good acoustically. When the Broadstairs Choral Society used it they erected a stand to take the complete choir at the back of the hall and reversed the seats for the audience. We did not have the resources to do this, since everything we collected was needed for charity, so we had to use the stage. It was difficult for tenors and basses at the back of the choir to project their voices through to the audience, but we had no choice.

That first concert was a remarkable success. True to their word, the chairman and the members of the council, with their families, duly appeared and sat in the front row. The hall was packed. No charge was made for admission but people could only enter if they bought a programme. This ensured that they would have the words from which to sing and, more important, would be able to learn some new carols, for I was determined to carry out that part of the project as well. We included the Christmas music from the *Messiah* as well as a variety of carols, new and old.

At last, with some apprehension, I suggested that the chairman and members of the council should sing one of the verses of 'God rest you merry gentlemen' alone. Taken by surprise and too disorganized to resist, they succumbed. The result was far from impressive and I never tried it again! Halfway through the programme we had a short interval for an appeal for the children in our convalescent homes and we brought the second half of the concert to a conclusion with *'Adeste Fideles'*. Everyone went home feeling rather better towards their neighbours, and the town – to judge from the reports in the local press – was thoroughly pleased with this new venture. This is how the Broadstairs Town Carol Concerts began.

—

The tradition of inviting well-known and popular guests to these events brought enormous pleasure to our regular supporters. In the early days at Broadstairs, the event that most lingers in my mind was when the actor Henry Ainley happened to be staying there and joined our party. He insisted on making his own contribution, and in a resonant voice read part of *A Christmas Carol* by Charles Dickens. This was particularly appropriate in the town that Dickens himself described as 'that agreeable watering place', where he spent so much of his time and wrote so many of his books.

When Sir Malcolm Sargent came he was, as ever, urbane, stimulating and witty in his comments. The audience loved it and the financial result was a record. But later, on the way back to London with some of our friends, he felt unwell, and on arrival at his home was rushed to hospital. It was, alas, the onset of the illness that was soon to prove fatal. I like to remember him full of fun and jollity, completely at ease singing carols with a local choir in a small seaside town, rather than as the stricken figure who just managed to appear to bid his farewell at the final night of the Proms in 1967. For the last twenty years of his life, Malcolm Sargent was probably the British conductor and musician best known to the public, particularly to the Promenaders, who adored him. In the world of professional music he was rather more controversial and there were always those ready to sneer. Perhaps as a result of his restless, nervous energy, he did conduct too many concerts a year; perhaps his repertoire of major works was somewhat limited; perhaps he did lack sympathy with the avant-garde products of contemporary music festivals; and perhaps he was snobbish in his approach to the non-musical world. For all that, he did a great deal to encourage British music and British musicians.

After making the appeal at the Town Carol Concert, Sir Malcolm wrote to me: 'Dear Ted, This is a quick "thank you" for a very happy day. You gave me a very happy luncheon and tea-party and I thoroughly enjoyed the concert. Your leadership was efficient, musical, persuasive and amusing – an ideal mixture for such occasions. All good wishes, Yours ever, Malcolm.' Perhaps because of his own early struggles, he always showed great kindness to others and readily supported causes in aid of musicians and others.

Another popularizer of a rather different kind is Joseph Cooper, who came down to the carol concert one Sunday afternoon to make the appeal. He took great pains beforehand to find out every detail about those we would be helping as a result of his appearance, and then demanded to know all about the audience. Finally, he asked me for how long he should speak, to which I replied: 'Four minutes or less, and five

minutes at the most.' In introducing him I recalled that I had first met him
when he was organ scholar of Keble College, Oxford, and later when he
was a cadet in the Royal Artillery Officer Training Unit at Shrivenham,
where he used to mount amusing and rather pointed revues, greatly
appreciated by the cadets. He was just completing his years at Keble when
I went up to Oxford; he left behind him a reputation for facility in every
realm of music and in particular a capacity for enlivening the chapel services, which at that time were compulsory for Keble undergraduates, by
basing his concluding voluntaries on popular themes of the day. Mention
of this proved fatal – perhaps I should say inspired! Having spoken his
carefully prepared words, Joseph Cooper could not then resist moving
the accompanist off the piano stool and treating the audience to his greatest work, a pastiche of a Bach Prelude and Fugue, based on the
well-known tune 'Today I feel so happy, so happy, so happy'. Lacking an
organ pedal board on the grand piano, he substituted the equivalent of a
tap dance with both feet and finally, carried away by enthusiastic recollections of his undergraduate days, brought the whole work to a shattering
conclusion with both hands and both feet, having taken up some twenty
minutes of our time. This met with tumultuous applause from the audience, who had thoroughly enjoyed themselves. The result showed in the
collection. It was marvellous to see Joe again at my eightieth birthday celebrations in 1996, still full of his customary wisdom and wit.

———

I conducted carol concerts at Broadstairs for forty years until they pulled
down the only hall where we could hold them. There was a movement
to have the concert in the local church, but we were always against this,
because people from other churches might not want to go there and
might think that we were supporting one particular religion or church.

As far as I was concerned, I thought we should be satisfied with forty years and call it a day. I was then asked to transfer my concerts to the constituency that I have represented since 1950, Old Bexley and Sidcup, and I agreed, provided all the proceeds went to charity and the concert was open to all. Just outside the constituency, we found a hall that would accommodate 1,500 people, but more than this wanted to come, so we had the concert over two nights. Over the years we have managed to keep a very good orchestra, made up mainly of people coming home to the area for Christmas. We have maintained the old traditions *in toto*, inviting a VIP to make an appeal on behalf of local good causes; and we still demand the participation of those in attendance!

CHAPTER THREE

A NEW WORLD?

———

W hen the Second World War came, I thought it was bound to
mean the end of music for me for some time to come. But it
did not quite. While awaiting my call-up for the Royal Artillery, I went
to the United States on a debating tour of American universities. It was
thought by the Foreign Office that this might help to put the British
position concerning our war objectives in a better light amongst our
contemporaries in America.

When I arrived in New York at the beginning of November 1939 one
of the first things I did was to go to the Carnegie Hall to hear John
Barbirolli conduct the New York Philharmonic Orchestra. We had been
very excited at home when Barbirolli had been chosen to succeed
Toscanini, then acknowledged as the greatest conductor of the world's
greatest orchestra. That night, Barbirolli began his programme with
Elgar's Introduction and Allegro for Strings. New York then was an exciting place for a young man to be – always busy, perhaps hard, but with a
bubbling Champagne-like quality to its life; in contrast, Barbirolli
brought some of the freshness and tenderness of the English countryside to the string playing of the New York Philharmonic in the Elgar
work, one of the best pieces for strings that he ever produced. There followed the Second Piano Concerto and the Overture to *Twelfth Night* by
Castelnuovo-Tedesco, neither of which have has the least imprint on my

mind; but then Barbirolli squeezed all the sensuality and vitality of which he was capable from Tchaikovsky's 'Romeo and Juliet' Overture.

That was the first time I heard Barbirolli conduct. Many years later, after he became conductor of the Hallé Orchestra in Manchester, I got to know him and his wife well. There was much to admire in his performances, particularly of Brahms, Mahler and Elgar, but towards the end of his life the loving care with which he always handled a work tended at times to distort its rhythm and structure. As a cellist himself, Barbirolli was able to obtain a deep warmth of tone from his players, which became an outstanding characteristic of all his orchestral work. Like Bruno Walter, he always wanted his orchestra to sing. At a concert in Manchester in his honour in the autumn of 1966 I heard him conduct the Hallé Orchestra in a rich, rhythmic reading of Brahms's Fourth Symphony. Afterwards I proposed his health, knowing full well that he had been taken ill on a number of occasions on the podium; in fact, I marvelled that anyone who burnt up his energy so furiously could go on living at the pace he was doing. When he died, I was presented with his baton case, battered and worn after its travels over so many years. It is a treasured possession.

But America also gave me another musical opportunity: the chance to hear jazz in its natural environment. Most people seem to have an automatic belief that if your interests lie in 'classical' music you cannot be bothered with 'light' music and will find jazz and any of its derivatives abhorrent. As a boy, however, I had been interested in any and every kind of music. When any of the well-known dance bands to which I listened on the radio, such as Jack Payne's, Jack Hylton's or Henry Hall's, came on tour to our part of the world, I made a point of going to hear them. I thoroughly enjoyed their rhythm, their precision and their

Above: Conducting carols in Broadstairs.

Below: Practising the piano in the Albany.

ABOVE: With Stokowski at the Royal Albert Hall.

BELOW: Rehearsing for 'that' concert, Royal Festival Hall, November 1971.

ABOVE: Music comes to Chequers, the country home of the Prime Minister.

RIGHT: Playing one of Europe's oldest organs, in Denmark.

Above: With William Walton and Peter Andry, then head of EMI Classics.

Left: With Maria Callas.

Right: Rehearsing Mozart with Gina Bachauer.

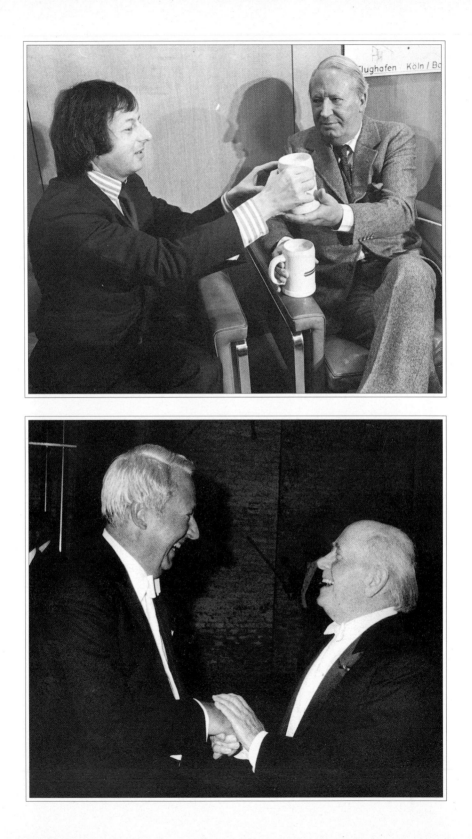

LEFT ABOVE: With André Previn, Köln-Bonn airport 1975.

LEFT BELOW: With Eugene Ormandy, Philadelphia 1976.

RIGHT AND BELOW:
Rehearsing for the launch concert of the first edition of this book, Music, *1976. I was clearly in trouble with Anneliese Rothenberger, but the problem seems to have been resolved!*

ABOVE: With Clifford Curzon in rehearsal, 1976.

BELOW: With Georg Solti (right) and Aram Khachaturian, January 1977.

arrangements of classical jazz numbers. In their way these large bands were the symphony orchestras of jazz; today we look on them as the coelacanths of the world of dance music.

Near Atlanta, Georgia, I heard my first Negro jazz band, its instrumentalists freely improvising as they worked the dancers up into a near frenzy. In Mobile, Mississippi, I listened to small groups playing the authentic 'blues', as one would expect from a town so close to New Orleans, where I heard much more of this kind of music in the early fifties. Back in the northern states, on New Year's Eve, 1940, in Cleveland, Ohio, I listened fascinated to Gene Krupa, probably the most brilliant drummer of all time, with his band, but so absorbed was I by his performance that I found it impossible to be interested in either the party or the dancing for which he was playing.

I have an intense admiration for the rhythmic vitality and powers of improvisation of those who play this music. I wish I had had the time to study more deeply its origins and to follow more closely the developments of recent years. Constant Lambert's *Music Ho!,* written in the thirties, deals wittily with the earlier periods of jazz and his work for piano and orchestra, 'The Rio Grande', which I often heard played at the Proms, was obviously influenced by his study of Negro music. This has now become a specialist world of its own but I see no reason why it should remain cut off from other spheres of music. Isolated attempts have been made to bring the two worlds together, but they will only be successful when there is infinitely more comprehension by both sides of the musical language they are using.

In Washington, DC, on the same visit, I saw *The Hot Mikado,* a jazzed-up version of Gilbert and Sullivan's opera. Many of those who have seen *The Black Mikado* in London and elsewhere must have been under the impression that this was the first time Sullivan had been treated in this way. *The Hot Mikado* of nearly sixty years ago was actually a far more original treatment of the opera. I already knew *The Mikado* well, for the D'Oyly Carte Company had brought the Gilbert and Sullivan operas to Oxford for a three-week season each year when I was a student. *The Yeomen of the Guard* has always been my favourite. What is there in any of them to beat that entrancing quartet 'When a wooer goes a-wooing'? In fact, I was – and still am – something of a Gilbert and Sullivan purist; what I have always wanted to see is the operas performed as Sullivan intended, cleaned of the accretions of a century and with their original orchestration. Malcolm Sargent did this from a musical point of view when he conducted the Company. Sir Charles Mackerras has followed the same practice in recent years. It seems to me a mistake to think that because they are popular, so-called 'light' music, the operas can be sloppily performed without detailed adherence to the composer's wishes. True, they have proved strong enough to withstand almost any treatment, but their performance requires just as high a technical standard as that of any other kind of music. As I held these views, *The Hot Mikado* certainly came as a shock; but I was then won over by the vitality and gaiety of the performance. This, of course, was in the days before electronics had reached their present high degree of amplification, when singers were still expected to project their own voices, and when we heard the natural sound of instruments. It is an interesting thought that the world of 'rock' music and all that has followed since would never have come about had it not been for the development of the electronic organ and the direct electronic amplification of the guitar. Without these, and particularly the latter, we should have been spared the ear-splitting noise that now so often permeates music of this kind; but, on the other hand, I doubt whether there would have been the same spur towards the exciting rhythmic developments which we have seen since the last war.

—

Back in England in early 1940 I was sent to a training camp at Storrington in Sussex, where I found Sir Arnold Bax ensconced in the local pub, the White Hart, for, as he said, the duration. Another trainee in the same barrack room was Robert Irving, later established in New York as a conductor of ballet. Whenever we could get to the White Hart there was the chance of some talk about music with Bax – whose 'Tintagel' ranks with the best of such tone poems, even matching Mendelssohn's 'Fingal's Cave' Overture – and we shared in the music-making that went on among his many visitors. Harriet Cohen, a dedicated Bach pianist, came frequently. One Sunday afternoon they even managed to get a quartet together to play Debussy.

Once posted to my regiment, however, I found there was little to do in the musical field except to conduct a dance band. Our resources were limited, but trumpet, saxophone, piano and drums gave us a basis on which to work. We had a signature tune – 'When you're smiling, when you're smiling, the whole world smiles with you' – and we always built up to a climax with our own arrangement of 'Tiger Rag'. I doubt whether the players really needed a conductor, but we provided support for many a visiting concert party and, musically, it was fun.

Travelling around in a regiment of artillery it was impossible to carry any of my own volumes of music and there were few public concerts in the towns we were defending, though I still have a programme for one in Preston in January 1942 when the London Philharmonic Orchestra under Edric Cundell played Brahms's Variations on a Theme of Haydn – which I had played in its two-piano form at school – and Beethoven's

Seventh Symphony. I read with envy of those who were able to go to Myra Hess's lunchtime concerts at the National Gallery. But when I was on a short leave near London I did hear the first performance of a work that has made a lasting impression on me, Vaughan Williams's Fifth Symphony in D. The Proms still continued in the Albert Hall, despite the bombing, and on 24 June 1943 I managed to get there for the concert beginning at 7 p.m. For once there was no question of queuing; the audience was thinly scattered about the hall. A note at the bottom of the programme explained that in the event of an air-raid warning we would be told immediately. Those of us who wished could take shelter, but the concert would continue. That night, Vaughan Williams, then over seventy, conducted his own work. None of us knew what to expect. His Fourth Symphony in F Minor, which had burst upon the world in 1935 with a ferocity quite unlike any of its predecessors, had immediately been interpreted as a commentary upon the strife towards which the world was undoubtedly heading. Was the Fifth to be an evocation of the war itself, or was it to be a commentary on it in human terms, filled either with despair or with the patriotic fervour of a previous generation? Vaughan Williams mounted the platform, almost stumbled his way through the orchestra, and there on the podium, bulky, slightly stooped, craggy, almost unkempt, he began the work. He had never been noted for his conducting, but the bareness and simplicity of his gestures seemed all of a piece with the nobility of the music that followed. Here was what we were searching for: spiritual refreshment at a time of strife, to remind us that the values we held dear were still what really mattered, despite what was going on outside. An air-raid warning had been given before the concert began, but all that slipped from our minds as we listened, absorbed, to this quiet, almost diffident restatement of faith.

As the last movement merged into the well-known chorale *'Lasst uns Erfreuen'* to which we normally sing 'All creatures of our God and King', with its recurring 'alleluias' – hope returned to us. We were not very many that night in the Albert Hall, but we had been present at a fresh flowering of Vaughan Williams's genius.

———

Having taken part in the campaign through France and the Low Countries, over the Rhine and across Germany, I found myself after VE Day commanding a battery that was in charge of a prisoner-of-war camp containing a German division just outside Hanover. The job given us by the Brigade Commander was to start clearing up the debris from the bombing and then to organize the rebuilding of the city – no mean task. When he gave me these instructions he added that he had one priority: the rebuilding of the racecourse so that those from the Armoured Cavalry regiments could indulge in their sport. He would allow me one priority. What was mine? I replied: 'The rebuilding of the opera house.' Not the main Opera House in Hanover, for that was beyond immediate reconstruction, but a small, charming eighteenth-century building at Herrenhausen on the edge of the city. Both priorities were quickly completed, and whether our interests were sporting or cultural, we were able to enjoy some relaxation from the almost continuous grind of the work we were doing. The first performance I saw at Herrenhausen was the usual double bill of *Cavalleria Rusticana* and *I Pagliacci*. For some reason in those early post-war days in Germany it seemed to be easier to get to hear opera than symphonic music. Later, in Osnabrück, I heard Mozart's *Seraglio* for the first time – admittedly a rough-and-ready performance on a stage in a barrack concert hall, in which the night before we had been listening to a concert party and singing 'Lili Marlene'. On a visit to Göttingen I was able to hear English operas that were not in the repertoire at home, Balfe's *The Bohemian Girl,* which contains the well-known soprano aria 'I dreamt that I dwelt in marble halls', and Wallace's *Maritana,* which has an equally popular aria, this time for the tenor, 'Yes, let me like a soldier fall'.

My interest in opera had been aroused when, as a boy of fourteen, I went to Paris with a small school party. There, at l'Opéra Comique on 19 April 1931 I saw Bizet's *Carmen.* It is difficult to think of an opera more suitable for a schoolboy, tuneful and colourful, stirring and yet full of tenderness. I say my interest was aroused because I always remember a girl who sat in the tier beneath me, who had continual difficulty in keeping in place the thin shoulder strap that alone held up her evening gown! I have seen *Carmen* many times since then. At the performance I saw in Barcelona, in July 1938, during my visit to Spain to observe the Civil War, many in the audience matched the cast in their colourful attire, despite the general drabness of the war outside. A horse on the stage in Act IV, however, looked distinctly underfed and rather scraggy. When the shot rang out in Act III we all automatically gripped the arms of our seats and prepared hastily to leave, then relaxed with a somewhat self-conscious laugh and settled back into our seats again.

—

After the war, living in London, it was to Sadler's Wells that I turned. It was cheaper than either Covent Garden or Glyndebourne, which for the time being I could not afford. At Sadler's Wells I could get to know opera in fairly intimate surroundings and at a reasonable cost, and if sometimes the productions did not match up to the highest standards, this gave me an insight into the problems of putting on an opera. There, too, I was able to cut my teeth on a wide-ranging repertoire, which included Johann Strauss's *Die Fledermaus,* Humperdinck's *Hänsel and Gretel* at Christmas time, Verdi's *Luisa Miller* – which I have never been able to hear anywhere else – Massenet's *Werther,* Tchaikovsky's *Eugene Onegin,* and Janáček's *Kátya Kabanová.*

On one occasion in 1953 I went back to Oxford for a performance of Delius's *Irmelin* at the New Theatre. I went not because I was particularly attracted by it but because I doubted – quite rightly, as it turned out – whether there would ever be a chance to hear it again. It is sad that none of Delius's operas seems to stand up on its own – not *Koanga,* nor *Irmelin,* nor even his *A Village Romeo and Juliet* – for there is lovely music in each of them. The radiance of 'The Walk to the Paradise Garden' from *A Village Romeo and Juliet* combines what is harmonically the most sensuous of Delius's shifting sound-textures with a sense of form that is sometimes lacking in his work overall. It is an intensely beautiful piece, and one of the most idiomatic examples of that peculiarly English brand of music where the strings produce that curious combination of intensity and timelessness. I conducted the piece at one of the concerts to celebrate my eightieth birthday, and the BBC Concert Orchestra played it superbly. The audience was evidently captivated – and, like so many listeners before them, no doubt conjured up images of a young couple walking, like Adam and Eve, into some enchanted and prehistoric garden. In fact, the 'Paradise Garden' is a pub – and the young couple make their way to it hand in hand, go upstairs and have a thoroughly energetic and enjoyable time! This must be so-called programmatic music at its most deceptive.

The suite from *Koanga* too has effective music, in its way fully comparable to Delius's smaller pieces 'On Hearing the First Cuckoo in Spring' and 'A Summer Night on the River'. Like many other composers,

Delius passed through a period of neglect after his death, all the greater perhaps because in his lifetime his supporters were so enthusiastic and his detractors so vicious, which in his case makes it more than usually difficult to strike a balance. Personally, I find 'Paris – The Song of a Great City' a powerful work; many were the times I looked out of the window of my room at the British Embassy in France during the European negotiations and listened to the true sounds of Paris; Delius's music always came back into my mind. But his *Sea Drift* and *A Mass of Life* still fail to inspire me.

What is the attraction of opera? Many people feel that they would like to enjoy it but are prevented from doing so because they feel that opera as an art form is artificial. True, it is; but then so is every other art form, even photography. At one time we spoke of a photographic reproduction; no one today would deny that the camera puts its own interpretation, or rather the interpretation of the photographer, upon its subject. But the artificiality of other art forms is acceptable; why is it not in opera? The problem with opera is that it needs an imaginative leap, from everyday life into a world in which people sing of their intentions and their emotions, and do so to an orchestral accompaniment. The leap becomes even more difficult when people in part sing and in part use the spoken word. Once that leap is made, however, once we accept intellectually and emotionally that in opera we are going to inhabit a world where things happen in this way, then the barrier disappears and we can share the enjoyment of some of the finest music ever written, splendid singing and good acting.

This of course is to brush aside the ever-attendant problems of poor scenery, outmoded costume, stilted production, bad lighting and foreign languages, to say nothing of singers whose voices may be well suited to their parts but whose figures leave much to be desired. In addition there is the complication of having an orchestra and conductor with lights over their music in front of the scene. Many of these problems are aspects of the quality of the performance, and the better we can make each of them, the more convincing the performance will be within the artificial world of opera in which we are moving. Then, too, there is the silliness of many of the stories on which the libretti of operas are based; but many a play on the modern stage has a story that is equally remote from reality. Indeed, a story far removed from our daily lives – for example that of Cinderella – may make it easier for us to enjoy our world of unreality.

Fortunately there has been an immense improvement in the last forty years in opera's presentation; designers now generally produce sets that are both practical and at the same time aesthetically appropriate; as a result of modern technology, producers can create almost any effect they may desire; singers now put a premium on their dramatic performances; and directors are determined to create a unity out of their work. What I still find disconcerting is that the spell is unnecessarily broken. Deep-seated, and probably unalterable, as the conventions are, I hate to hear applause for a singer interrupting the movement of the drama; I loathe to see the cast filing in front of the curtain at the end of each act, grinning and pumping one another's hands; and I dislike it equally when the mood of the last moments of the opera is immediately dispelled by the reappearance of the cast lined up on the front of the stage. All I want to see is the curtain lift on the final setting so that we remain under the spell when we applaud.

I have enjoyed opera more often at Glyndebourne than anywhere else in the world. John Christie's conception in the mid-thirties of a small opera house built on to his private home nestling in the Sussex Downs, where producers and singers could stay for six to eight weeks during the early summer with a permanent symphony orchestra to play for them, was an imaginative and determined attempt to achieve the highest standards of both musical and dramatic presentation in opera, particularly Mozart. He succeeded, probably beyond even his wildest dreams. It was not until 1953 that I was able to afford to go there and to enjoy Mozart opera beyond compare. To drive at leisure through the lovely Sussex countryside on a Sunday afternoon, to arrive at Glyndebourne in time to stroll around the gardens, looking at the white border and the blue border before coming to the lake, with the Downs standing out clearly against the early evening light, all setting the mood for an opera in the intimacy of the old house that seated only some 750 people; and to be able to spend the interval picnicking in the grounds, watching the cattle come up to the wooden fence, with all the fish jumping in the pool, still adds fun to the evening. Some people wondered whether John Christie was right to insist on people dressing up for the occasion. But that was the point; it was an occasion to which we, the audience, had to contribute. We knew, too, that on a Sunday it would not be an 'expense account' audience. Most of us had probably been saving for some time for this special occasion and we wanted to enjoy it to the utmost. When it was all over I would drive slowly back to London in the last light of a summer evening, the themes of the opera running again and again through my head; at times I could not help humming to myself or even bursting into song as the melodies of Mozart or the last pages of *Rosenkavalier* came back to me.

The new Glyndebourne Opera House, purpose-built under the leadership of John Christie's son George, is arguably the finest opera house in England. Like the Royal Opera House, it is probably at its best acoustically in the tiered seats higher up in the house – but the effect of the drama is best appreciated from closer in. There is no great lobby or bar, and there can be no opera house more airy or closer to the elements: leave most parts of the auditorium and you walk directly back into the world outside. The effect is similar to that of the Snape Maltings, where the design of the hall and the seating arrangements are also subservient to considerations of musical and dramatic effect. It is not as difficult to get tickets for Glyndebourne as some people seem to think, and I firmly recommend all music lovers to go at least once – perhaps starting with an autumn performance at the house by the excellent, and thriving, company of the Glyndebourne Touring Opera.

Rossini's *La Cenerentola* was the first opera I saw at the old Glyndebourne; it was conducted by Vittorio Gui, who at that time and for many years afterwards was the leading musical spirit there. Carl Ebert was the producer. Names that were to become so familiar were in the cast: Marina de Gabarain as Cenerentola, Juan Oncina as the Prince, Sesto Bruscantini as his valet. It was a delicious and enchanting performance; surely there could be no better introduction to operagoing than this fairy tale, unless it be one almost as popular each Christmas time, especially with children, Humperdinck's *Hänsel and Gretel*.

It is Glyndebourne that I have also to thank for my introduction to Richard Strauss: I saw *Ariadne auf Naxos* there the following year. Sena Jurinac sang the all-important part of the composer preparing the opera in the first act; Lucine Amara and Richard Lewis were Ariadne and Bacchus, and I heard Mattiwilda Dobbs and Geraint Evans for the first time, in smaller parts. The evening was cloudy and rain threatened. A picnic looked unlikely and we thought it prudent to put our hamper in the wooden hut near where we had parked the car. As we were settling in a splendid figure arrived to announce that he was the head scene-shifter and that we were occupying part of his property. He did not mind that, he said, and hoped we would enjoy the opera. When we were eating our supper during the interval he returned. 'Did I do well?' he asked. 'Yes,' we replied, 'we thought the scenery looked very good indeed.' 'No, no, no,' he said rather testily, 'I was the chap who walked across the stage at the end just before the curtain fell.' We had to confess that we had not recognized him in his performing role. Then he added: 'The last pages of this opera are some of the finest music which Richard Strauss ever wrote.' He was right. Whenever I hear it, the glorious love duet between Ariadne and Bacchus grips me until I can hardly bear to sit still in my seat. I want to share with them the ecstasy of Strauss's music. Together they mount the chariot, and as Strauss's swirling harmonies bring the opera to its conclusion we see the chariot with its twinkling lights disappear into the sky. At any rate that is how the production ended then; today the chariot usually advances towards the audience – a threatening gesture. I much prefer the lovers, in my make-believe world, to disappear among the stars. That is how I think of them as I drive home to the tunes of some of the most wonderful pages Richard Strauss ever wrote.

The next Strauss opera I saw at Glyndebourne was *Der Rosenkavalier*, the opera that made him famous. Its glorious melodies, its voluptuous orchestration, the never-flagging interest of the libretto, all these combined with superb voices, fine acting and an enchanting setting to exert a magic spell. *Der Rosenkavalier* has a special significance for me, for on a music stand in my home is a Strauss manuscript, and on one side of the sheet is a working sketch of the concluding bars of the first act of this opera in Strauss's small, meticulous handwriting. The notation on the other side, which was identified only with the help of Norman Del Mar, Strauss's biographer, is an early sketch for 'the solemn entry of the Knights of the Order of St John' for brass and timpani, composed in 1909. This manuscript was given to Mrs Asquith, the wife of the Liberal Prime Minister, by Richard Strauss at Garmisch on 12 May 1910 and inscribed by him to her. It later passed out of the hands of the Asquith family and was presented to me while I was Prime Minister. In response to a request from the Strauss family, I sent a photostat of the manuscript for the Strauss archives. I was delighted when, in return, Dr Franz and Frau Alice Strauss sent me the original of a letter from Richard Strauss to his wife posted from London on 23 June 1914 describing his meeting that day with the Prime Minister, Mr Asquith. After sixty years the connection between Richard Strauss and a British Prime Minister had been reconstituted. These personal possessions have given me a closer link with a composer whose work, not only his opera but also his tone poems and songs, I admire so much.

Those who enjoy *Rosenkavalier* will be eager to move on to Strauss's other works. The performances of *Salome* in October 1966 with Anja Silja in the title role showed how this opera can be transformed when Salome is personally – as well as musically – seductive. Equally, the lesser-known *Intermezzo,* in which the leading figure is the personification of Strauss's wife Pauline, requires an artist of real dramatic quality as a character actress, as well as a top-class soprano. Elisabeth Söderström, at Glyndebourne in 1975, showed that this combination can be triumphantly achieved. In 1976 Georg Solti led a production of *Die Frau ohne Schatten* at Covent Garden which was convincing in every way – and made me even more eager to see Strauss's works performed in Munich, in the opera house which, more than any other, is associated with the production of his operas. When I was taken round the opera house there shortly after it was reconstructed in the early sixties, I was envious to discover four full-sized revolving stages, each of which could be moved round to take centre stage – and above them a ballet rehearsal room the size of the full stage. Not only was there a splendid auditorium, but alongside it a full promenade, along which the audience could stroll and talk about the opera during the intervals – something that we have always lacked at Covent Garden. Now that the Royal Opera House is to be renovated at last, I hope that such considerations are all given the greatest priority: stagecraft of the highest order; a rehearsal space as similar to the performance space as possible; and a relaxed and comfortable atmosphere for the opera-goer. The new opera house at Glyndebourne has more or less satisfied all of these criteria, operating entirely in the unsubsidized sector – and the new Royal Opera House must not fall short, particularly given the likely scale of its Lottery grant!

—

Verdi's operas make an immediate appeal through their tunefulness. If to be able to whistle a tune after hearing it is a mark of a good piece of music, then Verdi succeeded better than most. His operas are as much a vehicle for the voice as a means of deploying a plot or revealing emotion. For me his two later works *Otello and Falstaff* are the ones that dramatically and musically give me most satisfaction. The performance of *Otello* which stands out in my mind is one I heard in the courtyard of the Doge's Palace in Venice in 1960. Played in the open air against a backcloth of St Mark's and the palace, a great stone staircase leading down into the courtyard, the opera had a spacious and splendid setting.

With Mario del Monaco as Otello, Tito Gobbi as Iago and Marcella Pobbe as Desdemona, it was magnificently sung. The scene was also very Italian. We began very late; the intervals were extraordinarily long; there were vociferous cheers after any good aria, or even a good top note, and when in the last act Emilia, Desdemona's lady, unfortunately fluffed one of her high entries, a loud groan swept across the audience. It was indeed a performance to remember, but afterwards everyone quickly nipped away to the bars in St Mark's Square to chatter once again about the ordinary things of life. I doubt very much whether that dramatic performance did much to purge the souls of those present!

I heard *Falstaff* for the first time at Glyndebourne, where in my mind it will always be associated with Geraint Evans. What a remarkable work it is for a composer in his eighties. The physical task alone of putting notes on paper for a major opera is enormous, quite apart from the mental effort required in the conception of the work and in maintaining its structure. Those who have come to enjoy Verdi's earlier operas will at first find it impossible to believe that *Falstaff* is the creation of the same man, so closely are the threads woven, both dramatic and musical, in the tapestry it presents. It is a mistake to think that *Falstaff* relies on its stage business to make its effect, for the more often one hears it and the more closely one is able to follow it, the more one sees that every stroke Verdi put on paper had its purpose in depicting the character of Falstaff and the actions of those around him.

I should like to think that in at least one sphere of musical activity we in Britain have attained standards that have been achieved nowhere else in the world; to my mind Mozart at Glyndebourne is an example of this. In 1956, the bicentennial of Mozart's birth, the Glyndebourne programme consisted of six Mozart operas, *Idomeneo, The Escape from the*

Seraglio, The Marriage of Figaro, Don Giovanni, Così fan tutte and *The Magic Flute* – a glorious enterprise that has never since been repeated. It was above all in order to present Mozart operas that Glyndebourne came into being, and no wonder, for taken as a whole Mozart's operatic *œuvre* is unmatched by that of any other composer. In endless hours of discussion, I have never resolved the argument as to which of Mozart's operas is the greatest. Perhaps it does not matter, for each contains such lovely music, each reveals aspects of human relations with which we are all familiar, and each contributes something to the enrichment of our lives whenever we hear it. *The Marriage of Figaro* has wit and style and, when well performed, a freshness that is alluring; *Don Giovanni* has strength, humour and a dramatically powerful ending; the *Seraglio* also has much humour, as well as Osmin's extraordinarily effective bass arias; while *Così fan tutte,* which Glyndebourne brought back into the world operatic repertoire, has a simplicity, charm and balance that in many ways make it the most appealing. At the tiny theatre in the Royal Palace of Drottningholm outside Stockholm in 1964, I saw a performance with Elisabeth Söderström and Kerstin Meyer in the leading roles, with the staging and costumes of Mozart's day. The orchestra too was in period dress. We in the audience sat on the wooden benches that were part of the opera house when it was built in 1766. By sheer good fortune, all these had remained unchanged while the opera house was used for other purposes in the intervening years. The modern restoration enabled us to enjoy *Così fan tutte* much as Mozart himself would have performed it. In contrast, it is not so easy to visualize the original production of *The Magic Flute,* for this is undoubtedly the most difficult of Mozart's works to stage, and puzzling too when one tries to plumb the depths of its symbolism. But none of this detracts from the majesty of the music.

Klemperer described it in his own programme note for a performance
I heard at Covent Garden as 'an incomprehensible cosmic work.
Everything is of the most sublime symbolism', and he then summed it
all up with the words: 'It is really not a comic opera – though sometimes
it seems so. Also it is not a mystery play – though it sometimes seems
so. It is only *Die Zauberflöte* of W.A. Mozart. That is enough.' How, then,
shall we say which of these works is the greatest? Let us be content that
Mozart gave us so much to enjoy today.

Beethoven, on the other hand, left us only one opera; but his *Fidelio*
is undoubtedly the greatest I have heard. Many may dispute this, but in
the majesty of its conception as well as in the splendour of its music it
means more to me than any other opera; and only Beethoven could have
handled so compellingly its twin themes of the triumph of freedom over
tyranny and of love over separation. I have seen many performances of
this opera, some of them thoroughly bad, yet the spiritual content of the
work always overcomes its inherent difficulties. To do *Fidelio* real justice,
of course, the cast must be outstanding. There must be no weak links.
Leonora must be a dramatic soprano of overpowering voice to be able
to manage Beethoven's great arias; Florestan, equally, must be a tenor
of high dramatic ability, especially when singing with Leonora in the
prison cell in the last act.

There are some who complain that Beethoven's structure tends to
break up the flow of the opera – this is very much a matter of production – and that his language is 'high-falutin'. But these defects, if defects
they are, are far outweighed by the quality of the music and the drama
itself. What could be more beautiful than the quartet in the first scene
of the first act, perfect in its melodic line, its clarity and its balance?
What more splendid than Leonora's great aria in the second scene? What

—

more emotional than the prisoners' singing as they slowly stumble into the daylight from their dungeons, their song swelling into a great cry for freedom? And is not Leonora and Florestan's duet in the dungeon one of the great love songs of all time? True, it is the transition from this to the general rejoicing over Florestan's release that so often provides an artificial ending to the opera, and it is here that the production needs to be more spontaneous so as to bring the opera to a natural end; even so, if the purpose of an opera is to provide drama to restate the eternal values of love and freedom, with music of a stature to mark them indelibly in our hearts and minds, then Beethoven's *Fidelio* is that opera.

Having said all this, however, I would still maintain that the greatest opera *performance* I have ever seen was of *Die Meistersinger* at the Salzburg Easter Festival of 1974, conducted and directed by Herbert von Karajan. With the best cast obtainable in the world at that time, with the full Berlin Philharmonic Orchestra in the pit, and with a stage containing every conceivable technical device, the splendid tale of the *Meistersinger von Nürnberg* unfolded before us. The settings were admirable and the action dramatic; it was only after the performance that I learned that in the fight at the end of the second act those flinging themselves from the attics or plunging into the pool were tumblers specially imported for the purpose. The final scene was one of colour and pageantry such as I had never seen before in an opera house, not even when Verdi's *Aida* was performed by La Scala at Munich during the 1972 Olympic celebrations. With a proscenium that could be narrowed or widened at will, the full width and depth of the stage were deployed, and the grey pilasters on either side themselves opened to display row after row of heralds. Throughout the performance von Karajan kept a firm grip on the whole structure and movement of the opera, and I for one found the impact of the final, glorious Prize Song almost overwhelming. Altogether it was a magnificent conception of the opera, superbly executed.

The audience at Salzburg, as at Bayreuth and many of the other major continental festivals, is drawn from all parts of Europe. We in Britain too should be proud of our common cultural heritage. When I returned to the Festspielhaus auditorium, just before the third act of *Die Meistersinger,* I was touched when the whole audience applauded, a tribute meant as a welcome to Britain's membership of the European family as much as to me personally. In Britain we would do well to encourage our fellow Europeans to come to our festivals, and to ensure that each in its own special way has an attraction to offer even the most critical of our European friends.

Moving to more modern times, Puccini's works are part of the staple diet of operatic life, be it *La Bohème, Madame Butterfly, Tosca:* all have glorious melody and excellent craftsmanship. The fact that they are so much part of the normal repertoire may be the reason why there is so seldom a performance that stands out. Individual artists do, however: Maria Callas and Tito Gobbi in *Tosca,* for example.

Benjamin Britten, more than any other modern composer, created his own operatic tradition and is recognized just as much outside Britain as within it. *The Turn of the Screw,* the first of his works that I saw, has left an indelible impression upon me, and I am delighted that *Peter Grimes* has gained in appeal as it has become more and more widely known and as his idiom comes to be accepted. Britten's last opera *Death in Venice* shows a remarkable use of instrumental colouring in the orchestra, combined with a maximum economy of means, but I am sure that the drama itself needed to be drastically pruned to make its real impact. I heard one of the first performances of William Walton's *The Bear* at the Aldeburgh

Festival. This is a delightful and witty work, which ought to become part of the intimate opera repertoire. No one could say that any of these are 'avant-garde' works.

—

Festivals have long played a part in English musical life. Most of the older ones were based primarily on choral singing. The oldest, celebrating its 270th anniversary in 1997, is the Three Choirs Festival of Worcester, Gloucester and Hereford. Each year, in its setting in one of these cathedral towns, it induces an atmosphere of amiable music-making in which the cathedral organists play the leading part, the cathedral choirs sing Daily Services and the choral works are sung by amateurs who join together for this purpose, supported by one of the London or provincial orchestras. These are festivals I always enjoy, not only for the music-making but for the talk that goes on over a meal or a drink late into the night. Traditionally, there is always one of the great choral works of Bach, Mendelssohn, Elgar, Vaughan Williams or Mahler, as well as those by more contemporary composers such as Walton, Britten, Franz Reizenstein and Kenneth Leighton. They achieve their purpose by enabling us to enjoy and talk about music; I doubt whether they would claim to put on performances of the same standard as can only be achieved by permanent and professional choirs and orchestras.

Today, while some of the older festivals in our great cities like Leeds and Birmingham have lost their prominence, the new post-war festivals have established themselves mostly in smaller places and in different forms. Very often they were created by an outstanding musical personality who influenced their nature and their programmes, and around whom much of the festival revolves. This was always the case with Benjamin Britten at Aldeburgh, but the festival has proved its lasting worth by thriving for the past twenty years despite the death of its founding light. Indeed, it is now ten years since the death of Peter Pears, and the legacy continues to flourish. It seems that every year the Aldeburgh Festival can still find at least one of Britten's works that can be completed and brought to performance for the first time – or a forgotten work that can be performed again and reappraised. Perhaps the best examples have been some of the works that Britten wrote in the thirties and forties for the BBC: the Radio Cantata 'The Company of Heaven' includes another rapturously beautiful setting of the great hymn tune set by Vaughan Williams in the finale of his Fifth Symphony, and is well worth hearing.

The one festival that unquestionably outshines all individual influences is that of Edinburgh, which provides as comprehensive a programme of music, opera, ballet and drama, together with exhibitions of paintings and other treasures, as any festival in the world. In addition, it has what in my experience is a unique feature, the Fringe activities – such as music and drama from our universities and many other groups, usually put on outside festival hours, either to provide revues and other forms of light entertainment or to give us the opportunity of seeing experimental theatre and hearing avant-garde music.

Edinburgh, as a city, with the castle in the background and its beautiful unspoilt squares, provides a venerable setting for a festival. In the eighteenth century its cultural activities were as lively as those of any city in Europe. Over time the festival has helped to re-create Edinburgh as a natural centre for the arts. I must confess, however, that what I have probably enjoyed more than anything at Edinburgh is being able to bring the musical establishment and the Fringe together, either at drinks or over a meal. Until I did so, in 1965, when I was Leader of the

Opposition, never the twain had met. At their first encounter they did little more than stare rather fixedly at each other, but after that it became a common experience and each side realized it had much to gain from the other. Of course, it is bound to be a rather one-sided business, for while the establishment continues in possession, the Fringe changes almost year by year, and only slowly does it become absorbed into the establishment itself. Nevertheless, I have always felt it a good thing that each should influence the other. At any rate, there is something for everybody at the Edinburgh Festival, and for those who want to explore music with the opportunity of seeing a play, looking at pictures or going to a show with a little light, if somewhat scurrilous, relief at the end of the day, Edinburgh is the festival with which to start.

—

Ballet may appeal to some as a more natural way than opera of enjoying music and drama together. The barrier of artificiality is perhaps less formidable: it is after all natural for human beings to dance to express their emotions. Perhaps, too, some trace of what occurred in olden tribal days – whether at times of planting or at harvest, whether in wooing or in marriage, whether in preparation for war or celebration for peace, whether in birth or in death – still lies deep within us: many might say that this more primitive spirit is now breaking out again in the contemporary dancing of our young people. At any rate it does seem true that we can respond more easily to ballet than to opera. The music is easier on the ear – what can be more attractive than Tchaikovsky's ballet music for *The Sleeping Beauty* and *The Nutcracker,* or Delibes's for *Coppélia,* or the arrangement of Chopin's pieces for *Les Sylphides?* And the figures are easier on the eye – what can be more satisfying than the *corps de ballet* moving gracefully as one in *Giselle?* I have never become an expert on the technique of ballet, but then I have never found that necessary for my enjoyment of it. While I am sure that technical knowledge does contribute to the pleasure of those who have it, what I look for is simply beauty of movement, harmonization of music and dance, and expression of emotion and character by the dancers. When I see a performance embodying all three, it gives me deep satisfaction.

Looking back over the post-war years, two events in dance stand out in my mind, not altogether unrelated. The first was the arrival of the musical *Oklahoma!* at Drury Lane in London in April 1947. That was a revelation. In Britain we were still suffering from the after-effects of the war, rationed and constricted, tired and strained. That American company of dancers brought to *Oklahoma!* a vitality and colour that we had not seen for years. And when, after the final curtain, far from disappearing to their rooms, the curtain lifted again and we saw them dance each theme song off the stage, we marvelled that any group could have such dynamism and energy. Perhaps *Oklahoma!* did more than anything to show many of us what was still possible in life on the stage. The second event was the first visit of the Bolshoi Ballet from Moscow to London in 1956. Then it was Prokofiev's *Romeo and Juliet* which we found quite staggering. Never before had I seen such beautiful dancing on the stage, such precision in the *corps de ballet,* such power and strength in the men and such support from the orchestra pit. That opened my eyes to what ballet could really be like. No subsequent visit of the Bolshoi has made anything like the same impact, perhaps because our own standards have risen so fast, perhaps because the Bolshoi itself appears to have lost its capacity to move forward with its productions, even though its dancing is still of a very high order. On its second visit, in 1963, it was Prokofiev's *Lieutenant Kijé* – a big contrast to *Romeo and Juliet* – which made its mark. The tale of a soldier who never exists, but because of an ink blot on an official paper has to be created and eventually disposed of, is itself ludicrous; the music I find intrinsically funny. Well produced, the ballet is at times hilarious and at other moments deeply emotional, and it appears to be the nearest the Bolshoi Ballet has got to the many modern character ballets danced so well by our own Royal Ballet.

When the Bolshoi Ballet came to London for the second time I was Lord Privy Seal at the Foreign Office. On the Friday before the Monday on which they were due to open at Covent Garden, the Soviet Minister of Culture, Madame Furtseva, sent me a message saying that she had decided to accept my invitation to be present and would stay for a week. Despite this rather short notice, I was delighted to be able to entertain her and immediately prepared a programme of artistic and cultural activities to show her what the British could do. The opening night was a great success, and we went to the ballet almost every night that week. I was somewhat disconcerted to find, however, that every day the rest of her programme was being cancelled. The final blow came when my Private Secretary told me on the Wednesday evening that a messenger had arrived from Madame Furtseva to enquire about Henry Moore, whose studio in Hertfordshire she was due to visit the following day. 'Was he a modern sculptor?' he enquired; to which the inevitable answer was 'Yes'. 'Did that mean that his sculpture had holes in it?' he further enquired. The answer was clearly in the affirmative. 'In that case it would be quite improper for a Soviet Minister of Culture to pay a visit to Henry Moore's studio'; furthermore, he added, 'I think it would be better if we cancelled the arrangements for the rest of the week.'

On hearing this, I asked my Private Secretary to send a message to say that I would go to the Soviet Embassy myself on Friday morning, at

10 a.m., in order to look after the Minister of Culture personally for the day. Madame Furtseva accepted this arrangement. I took her first to the Royal College of Music, where the end-of-term examinations were in progress, and then to the Wallace Collection. Before lunch, we called in at my flat at Albany. Madame Furtseva asked whether flats like that were provided for all Ministers and Members of Parliament. Regretfully I told her that all except three Ministers had to find their own homes and pay for them. She was astonished, but then said rather wistfully: 'In all the visits that I have made to London, this is the first time that I have been in anyone's home.' For lunch, we went to Wimbledon, saw an afternoon's play and then returned for the ballet. I felt that I had taken a firm grip on the situation and I had shown the Soviet Minister of Culture some sides of British life that she had never seen before.

That evening at Covent Garden remains in my memory, not so much because of the ballet, which I had already seen, as for the conversation Madame Furtseva and I had with some of those responsible for the production during the second act. I asked them when the Bolshoi would put on Stravinsky's *Firebird* or *Petrushka*. This led to an animated discussion as to whether Stravinsky had now become doctrinally acceptable in the Soviet Union. The debate ranged to and fro between the question of Stravinsky's own attitude towards the Soviets and that of whether the ballet music he had written before the Revolution was in fact compatible with the cultural ideals now held by those in authority. I listened fascinated to this ideological battle over what was to me purely a practical question. Feeling quite inadequate to intervene, I could only wait while those taking part came to the tentative conclusion that provided Stravinsky meantime did not commit any heresies, it might well be possible for the Bolshoi in a few years to start making preparations for a production of *Petrushka.* On that note of reconciliation we went back to our box.

The first performance of *Ondine,* with music by Hans Werner Henze and danced by Margot Fonteyn and Michael Somes, was one of the major events at the Royal Ballet in my experience. Apart from Henze's remarkable music, whose soft, surging sound seemed to carry the ballet along, Fonteyn and Somes gave brilliant performances. They had to, for *Ondine* is a full-scale work which requires the highest technical accomplishment from its dancers. It is a pity that it is so difficult for a major work of this kind to make a permanent home in the repertoire, as opposed to the shorter ballet, which may be combined with others without putting at risk a whole programme. Surely *Ondine* deserves a permanent place, not only for its music but for its choreography and its setting.

—

The rapidly growing appreciation of music in Britain – once contemptuously known as 'the land without music' – particularly among young people, owes a great deal to radio and television, as well as to the imaginative teaching of music in our schools and universities.

For many years I drove up from my home on the coast to the House of Commons every Monday morning. I tried to time it so that I could stop for coffee on the motorway and get back on the road again just before 10.30. I could then listen to Antony Hopkins for half an hour, week by week, talking about a composer or a work from that week's broadcasts. From him I learned a great deal during those years, not least about Schoenberg's early works. On one occasion this proved to be a vastly expensive half-hour. Hopkins spent the entire programme dilating most persuasively on Charles Ives, the American composer, little of whose work I had then heard. He played Ives's setting of the 90th Psalm, which came as a complete discovery to me. I found it profoundly moving, and when I reached London I did not even go to the House of Commons, but drove straight to the Army and Navy Stores and bought every recording of Ives's works they had in stock. I have played them many times since, but I have yet to find Ives himself quite so persuasive! Nevertheless, I shall always be grateful to Hopkins for having first led me to his setting of the 90th Psalm.

Although, as André Previn first showed back in the seventies, television can be a useful educational medium, I do not think it will ever quite match the full magic of a live musical performance for me. The effectiveness of any broadcast depends, of course, on the quality of the direction and above all on the quality of the sound. But however accomplished these are, there will always be natural limitations to this format: to carry the entire stage on screen makes the performance seem remote and too small to be convincing; to focus on individual singers or players detracts from the balance of the production and makes them seem unrelated to the rest of the performance. Although technology seems to have improved exponentially during the past twenty-five years, these fundamental shortcomings remain: in an ideal world there is nothing quite like a live performance, seen and heard in the flesh.

I have had the privilege of knowing many fine musicians, but amongst the finest were Herbert von Karajan and Leonard Bernstein. As well as being hugely charismatic and musically brilliant, they shared a fascination with the potential of advancing technology. Many of their concerts, dating back to the seventies, were filmed in order to be released when the already foreseen home-video market took off on a large scale. Generally, Lenny Bernstein's concerts would be recorded live for CD and video release, whereas von Karajan on the whole preferred studio recordings

– directing the cameras as well as the orchestra. The effect of these is tremendously powerful, with the ranks of Berlin string players moving together, almost like a single organism and usually arrayed on an angular set designed to distract the eye as little as possible. In Vienna, Bernstein's concert video recordings of the Mahler symphonies have been played as a cycle on a huge screen opposite the city Rathaus. I am told that these were sell-out occasions – and, of course, this is sadly the only way now of seeing this great musician make music.

I am sure that the possibility of high-fidelity sound on television and video has completely altered most people's perception of music on television. Twenty years ago I had no doubt at all that radio was a medium far to be preferred for music. Until comparatively recently, it was often embarrassing to witness a conductor's theatrical exhortations and an ululating orchestra's best efforts accompanied by a scarcely audible, muddy soundtrack – and the direction too was primitive in the early days of television broadcasting from the concert hall.

Perhaps the greatest problems in televising music have arisen when a choir is involved. A close-up of an array of mouths opening and shutting is not particularly attractive for the viewer. I remember a television recording of Berlioz's Requiem Mass conducted in the church of Les Invalides in Paris by Leonard Bernstein. I admit that I have always thought this work to be overrated: the Sanctus for tenor solo is a lovely piece of writing, but the rest fails to thrill me. With this performance I remember most vividly how off-putting the contrast was between the energy displayed by Bernstein in his endeavours to produce a tremendous impact and the stolidity of the response in front of him – additionally muffled by the vast acoustic of the church.

With the advent of NICAM stereo, laser discs and simultaneous broadcasts between television and radio, matters have improved a great deal technically. Although direction can still be obtrusive and distracting, opera in particular has become more readily available thanks to television – and the broadcasts from Glyndebourne are an outstanding example of how simultaneous broadcasting can be both superbly done and extremely popular. Television broadcasts from the Proms are another thriving tradition – the Last Night is now broadcast right across Europe and beyond – which enables the armchair viewer to experience fine music.

Perhaps there is now a generation that actually prefers to watch its sport, its music and much else besides entirely over the airwaves – and perhaps we can now appreciate how far-sighted those great musicians were to leave their legacy for the future in a multi-media form. It should certainly be a cause for celebration that future generations will see something of the art of these great men, as we have long treasured the few flickering images of conductors such as Reiner and Toscanini making music. It would, however, be a great irony if the main effect of this enthusiasm for technology were to be a decline in live music-making. I hope that recorded and broadcast music will go on being an introduction to the real thing – and not a substitute for it.

—

In the first edition of this book , I wrote that 'Music of all kinds in Britain is flourishing as never before.' In many ways, this is still the case. Since 1976, truly magnificent concert halls have sprung up in various parts of the country – notably St David's Hall in Cardiff, Symphony Hall in Birmingham and Manchester's replacement for the Free Trade Hall, the Bridgewater Hall – and a combination of the CD revolution and the appeal of Classic FM have made classical music far more accessible.

Certainly, all of this means that more resources are going into classical music in Britain. The balance between the amount of public money going to national organizations and the amount going to the regions will always be a difficult one to strike. Those outside London naturally tend to think of themselves as being deprived of essential cultural activities, and consider that those in London benefit at their expense. Personally, I still think the main problem is that those who live by disbursing taxpayers' money are always over-fond of settling policy on doctrinal or ideological grounds, which hardly enhances creativity.

Of course, one particular comparison between London and other great musical cities is remarkably telling: London simply has far more orchestras than any other city in the world. We have five symphony orchestras, plus the BBC Concert Orchestra, the English Chamber Orchestra, the London Mozart Players, the Academy of St Martin-in-the-Fields, the Academy of London and any number of smaller ensembles, including the excellent London Sinfonietta. But few of the players really enjoy what might be regarded internationally as proper conditions of service – with the exception of the London Symphony Orchestra, whose well-established residency at the Barbican has been so fruitful. But even the LSO, our most financially secure orchestra, is sometimes expected to play three different programmes in a week – often under a visiting maestro.

Other international cities with the highest musical standards and the best-established audiences generally try to support only one first-class symphony orchestra, often alongside – at most – a highly professional but by no means world-class radio orchestra and a couple of chamber orchestras. This is true of Vienna, of Paris, of Berlin, and of the big American cities. Each orchestral programme is likely to have been intensively rehearsed for a week or so, and then will be played three, or perhaps four, times in the concert hall.

Seldom do British orchestras, however, have more than one full rehearsal in the hall of the concert; many have none at all. Rehearsals for a single concert can take place in three or more different locations. Our players may be the best sight-readers in the world, but how can we ever expect them to reach the heights of the Viennese or the Berliners when they are forced to operate like this? I do not know what the full-time, core membership of each of our orchestras is, but I am now well used to seeing the same faces when conducting supposedly quite different bands.

All this is further complicated by the fact that we have such a substantial capacity for training musical students, most of whom naturally wish to work subsequently as musicians. The supply of talented musicians seems to be endless, yet classical concert-going remains predominantly the province of an ageing, white and middle-class audience, and the demographic trends are not wildly encouraging.

London is a great musical city, but there must be some rationalization. We need to think of our musical life not as a series of competing, financially unsound empires, but as one great Performing Arts Centre, where only the highest standards will do. So much is right about London, particularly the pool of talent that we have amongst our orchestral musicians, that we really must be able to make better sense of our concert life. Unless at least two or three of our orchestras merge their resources, I cannot foresee the emergence of a London 'super-orchestra' that could really challenge at the top of the International Orchestral Premier League. There are signs now that the LSO, thanks to their excellent music directors in recent years, their generous sponsorship from the City of London and their loyal audiences, might be about to prove me wrong. In a way, I hope that they do – but I am still not convinced that the highest standards of excellence can be maintained in London.

I know that there are many demands on taxpayers' money, but I am quite sure that the comparatively small amounts that are spent on the arts produce financial benefits alone that justify every penny – and the non-financial benefits simply cannot be quantified. Now that the rules on distributing Lottery proceeds have been altered to allow contributions to current spending as well as capital, the potential exists for a complete rejuvenation of our musical life. I hope that we seize it, because we cannot take it for granted that the unrivalled musical foundations that we still enjoy will be there indefinitely if we, as a society, go on neglecting them.

CHAPTER FOUR

HARMONY
AT No. 10

——

When I moved into 10 Downing Street as Prime Minister, it was to become my home. I had no other. Moreover, when people came there I wanted them to feel not that they were coming to an office with an official residence and a flat over it, but that they were coming to a home with an atmosphere just like their own. In my early days as a Member of Parliament I had seen No. 10 when Sir Winston and Lady Churchill lived there; in her inimitable way Lady Churchill had imbued the building with her own personality. The state rooms were not just there for official purposes; they were lived in daily and were part of the Churchills' family life. The Churchill pictures and treasures were on display in the drawing rooms. The same was true of the occupancies of Sir Anthony and Lady Eden and of Harold and Lady Dorothy Macmillan, though possibly to a lesser extent in the case of the Macmillans because Lady Dorothy so adored the country and her garden and house in Sussex that she found it difficult to drag herself away from them.

The No. 10 staff liked to think of themselves as one family working together and, indeed, so closely were we brought into contact in this small building that it was essential for the effectiveness of our work that we should live happily together. In this we were helped by the fact that we were a small group. The Prime Minister's office at No. 10 must be one of the smallest for any head of government in the world. When I first visited the White House and found that the staff totalled over 1,100, I realized how tiny we were. In all, private secretaries, the secretaries, the typists, those who looked after the Prime Minister's patronage, including honours and ecclesiastical appointments, those who answered the mail from the general public running to roughly 100,000 letters a year, those who looked after security, the telephonists, the messengers, and those who cleaned the building, added up to only eighty-three. It was difficult for anything to happen to anyone in the family without the others being affected. I too wanted to make No. 10 a real home – and for me home meant music.

One of the best-known photographs taken at the time I became Prime Minister showed my Steinway piano being moved into No. 10. After the breakdown of the first negotiations for Britain's entry into the European Community, through President de Gaulle's veto in January 1963, I had been awarded the Charlemagne Prize by the city of Aachen for my work in trying to create a wider European unity. With the prize money I bought a small rosewood grand piano from Steinway's which had recently completely renovated it. Built in 1922, it came from a vintage year – for pianos have good and bad years just like wines. Moura Lympany, the concert pianist, helped me to choose it. We toured the piano stores of London together, she playing to demonstrate every aspect of a piano's capabilities while I listened. At first I attempted to find a Bösendorfer, knowing Donald Tovey's insistence on this make, but they are now few and far between and I finally settled on the Steinway. It was the first time I had had a piano of my own; until then I had relied on the one bought from Thornton Bobby's, nearly forty years before, which was at my father's house at Broadstairs, or on hired instruments.

The Steinway was placed in a corner of the White Drawing Room on the first floor at the corner of No. 10 looking out over both Horse Guards Parade and St James's Park. It was the first time a piano had been permanently installed in the house since Arthur Balfour had ceased to be Prime Minister in 1906. Whenever an opportunity occurred I could easily get there for a few minutes' practice, particularly after a quick tray lunch or in the early evening after the day's meetings were over; often I would play late at night when I got back from official functions or from the House of Commons. My Principal Private Secretary once said to me that whenever they could hear the Steinway at No. 10 they all heaved a sigh of relief, knowing that for a brief time at least the demands made upon them would slacken. It was true that afterwards I would return refreshed and ready for the fray, but those interludes were beneficial for all of us.

Another instrument that played an important part in musical life at No. 10 was the clavichord in the drawing room in my flat at the top of the building. This marvellous instrument was made for me by Tom Goff, the creator also of many modern harpsichords, who not only specialized in the construction of the instrument but also executed the beautifully inlaid decorative casing. Even among musicians comparatively little is known about the clavichord. When Giulini was in London to conduct the Beethoven *Missa Solemnis* in St Paul's Cathedral, he came to No. 10 so that we could talk together about the Mass for Italian television. We did so alongside the Steinway. Afterwards he said he had heard that I had some excellent stereo equipment, which he would like to hear. I took him up to the sitting room of my flat, where I had it installed, and put on a record of the Amadeus Quartet playing a Haydn quartet. After listening to the first movement he said that he had never heard such pure reproduction of musical sound. I had taken great trouble over this equipment, using the best individual components I could find from different sources. In particular I had spent a considerable time listening to different makes of loudspeaker before finally settling on electrostatic ones. Even then I had had the normal wooden framework replaced with a chromium one, the speakers themselves re-covered with different material and each speaker placed on rollers for easy positioning. As Giulini said, the total effect in purity of reproduction was remarkable. Without telling him what I was doing, I put on the Sanctus from his own recording of the Verdi Requiem. He listened for a few moments and his eyes lit up and his face broke into a broad smile as he said excitedly: 'That is *my* music.' Then he turned towards the instrument by the window and asked: 'What is that?' 'My clavichord,' I replied, as I moved to open the lid. 'What is a clavichord?' he asked, to my astonishment. I reminded him that Johann Sebastian Bach had written forty-eight preludes and fugues for the 'well-tempered clavier'. This was a clavier. 'I have never seen such an instrument before,' he commented, as he gently touched the keys. The clavier is a small instrument covering only just over four octaves, roughly half the range of a piano. The strings are touched from below by pieces of metal. There is, of course, no sustaining or damping pedal. Its main limitation is perhaps its quietness, but this has its own value: when the clavichord is played, it imposes a special silence on its surroundings and induces a quite remarkable peace of mind.

The best example of this in my experience came when I was taking part in recording the Oscar Peterson show in a large BBC studio in London containing an audience of some 300 people. After Oscar Peterson had displayed his own virtuoso technique and we had discussed together our common interest in music, he asked me to play something on my clavichord, which had been brought down to the studio for this purpose. I had previously checked with my tuner that all was well – tuning is affected, of course, by movement as well as by the temperature and humidity of the surroundings – and I had also asked whether the amplification was satisfactory, but I had not had an opportunity to test it in the studio before the interview. Having been told that the amplification was all right, I assumed that the clavichord was being amplified for the whole studio, from which the television sound would then be taken for the audience at home. But as soon as I began to play Bach's First Prelude in C Major I realized my mistake. The amplification was going direct to the control panel and all that the studio audience was getting was the natural sound of the clavichord. Even so the instrument imposed its own silence. I could sense the intensity of this listening audience as I played and, as I found afterwards, in some extraordinary way the sound carried to everybody in that hall.

Another outstanding non-classical musician whom I met at around this time was the late Duke Ellington, who brought his band to play at a concert of sacred music in Westminster Abbey. This was a brave attempt to play some of the music derived from Negro spirituals in a religious setting: it certainly created a different atmosphere for the enormous crowd that thronged the Abbey. But the 'Sacred Concert' especially written for the event by Duke Ellington had only been completed a few hours before, the music was under-rehearsed, and the old maestro was already ailing. Although he came on to No. 10, he was too tired to stay for supper. Despite all that, I knew that I had spent a couple of hours in the presence of one of the greats.

The memory of one moment at the clavichord will always remain of supreme importance to me. On Thursday 28 October 1971, the House of Commons finished its long series of debates on Britain's proposed membership of the European Community. The negotiations had been successfully settled after my meeting with President Pompidou in Paris in May of that year. At the end of the debate came the vote. I was delighted with the unexpectedly large majority of 112. This was the result of sixty-nine Members of the Opposition Labour Party defying their party's three-line whip, standing by their principles and voting with us for Britain's entry into Europe. For me it was the culmination of ten years' continuous work, argument, organization and negotiation. It was a triumph for all who had devoted so much time and energy to the European cause in which they so strongly believed; the opening of a new era for Britain and for Europe. Naturally, everyone wanted to celebrate and the champagne was ready to flow. The demands of the media for immediate appearances on radio and television were insatiable. I felt I wanted none of these. For me the significance of that moment was too great either for off-the-cuff reaction or for the popping of corks. With just a few friends, those who had been closest to me throughout all this time, I went quietly back to No. 10 and up to my sitting room. There, as they stood by, I played Bach's First Prelude and Fugue for the Well-Tempered Clavier. The clavichord had its effect: after ten years of struggle and setbacks, in success it gave us peace of mind.

The Steinway, the clavichord and the stereo were my own personal ways of making music, but I wanted music to enter more widely into the life of No. 10. There were many ways in which this could be done. I began by introducing sung graces before and after meals when I entertained official visitors. This was in the great dining room, a splendid panelled room with seating for some sixty to seventy guests around its horseshoe-shaped table. Acoustically, the room is excellent – clear and not too resonant. The only disadvantage was one I had known ever since I first dined there as a young member of Mr Churchill's government at his Eve of Session Dinner in October 1951, nearly twenty years before. The walls were hung with portraits of great men, Pitt and Fox, Nelson and Wellington, but though the sitters were great, the pictures them- selves were copies of an inferior kind. For twenty years, whenever I had lunched or dined in that room, I had thought how incongruous it was, when the nation possessed so many enviable treasures, that heads of gov- ernment and other distinguished visitors who sat at the British Prime Minister's table should look around and see nothing but copies. In time I was able to change all this. The dark panelling was stripped and light- ened, the dining room redecorated and refurbished in keeping with it and the copies on the wall replaced by four great Gainsboroughs and two Romneys, kindly lent by those sympathetic to my ideas. It was then a perfect room for music.

A group of singers led by Martin Neary, the organist of St Margaret's, Westminster, the House of Commons church, would come on each occasion to sing grace and I soon asked them if they could put together a programme of madrigals and part-songs for us to listen to after din- ner, while we drank our coffee and liqueurs. This they did admirably, to the great delight of our guests. They soon began picking a programme to suit each individual occasion. Martin Neary did a great deal of dig- ging around in old folios of music, and we all had a lot of fun selecting from the results of his research. Mostly it was a case of finding words that bore some pointed relationship to the occasion in question, and when the time came we all watched to see the impact of these on our guests' faces. I well remember the reactions of Mr Whitlam, the then

Prime Minister of Australia, and his wife, when – unannounced – the singers burst into their own arrangement of 'Waltzing Matilda'. I noticed husband and wife exchange glances across me, with raised eyebrows – 'Do these people think this is the Australian National Anthem?' I thought they might be wondering, for this was an issue of violent controversy in Australia at the time.

Perhaps the most moving of all these occasions was when I entertained at 10 Downing Street the representatives of Northern Ireland and the Republic of Ireland, who were taking part in negotiations at Sunningdale over the establishment of the future relationship between the two countries. At the end of the first day's conference I had invited them all to dinner, but for reasons of security no one had been told where this would be, only that they would leave Sunningdale at seven o'clock; to their surprise they soon found themselves at No. 10. There had been no gathering like it in Downing Street before. For me it was an emotional moment. I was able to bring together round the same dinner table the representatives of those who had spent so many centuries quarrelling with Britain or with each other. Now at last a settlement seemed to be within our grasp. I was touched when John Hume and Paddy Devlin, two of the Social Democratic Labour Party representatives from Northern Ireland, came up to me and said: 'We never expected to be inside No. 10 tonight. The last time we were at No. 10 we were lying on the pavement opposite in a protest demonstration and no one so much as gave us a cup of tea.' Then one of then added: 'And what's more it rained all night, so in the morning we packed it in.' I had asked Martin Neary to abandon the usual programme of madrigals and choose familiar songs that would appeal to our guests. Once the singers started there was no holding back the Irish. They immediately joined in and by the end of the evening they had taken over completely. The lilt of 'When Irish eyes are smiling' spread round the room. They went back to Sunningdale feeling better towards each other — and even perhaps towards the British.

We were also able to use the dining room for chamber music concerts. The first was a most unlikely occasion. The Amadeus Quartet played the Haydn Quartet, Opus 76 No. 1 in G Major and the Schubert Quartet in A Minor to celebrate the first issue of a new Central Statistical Office publication, *Social Trends*. As Mrs Muriel Nissel, the first editor of *Social Trends,* is the wife of the second violin in the Amadeus Quartet, the connection was not as tenuous as it appears at first sight. The audience was made up in part of those concerned with social developments whom we thought might be interested in music, and those known to us as musicians whom we considered might become involved in these social matters. The Quartet played beautifully, throwing off the Haydn with light-hearted zest and bringing out all the depths of feeling in the Schubert. The dining room gave them a clear, bright tone. The same quartet played again for me in November 1972 at a reception I gave for the committees organizing the Fanfare for Europe, the celebrations for Britain's entry into the EEC, due to take place in January 1973, but on this occasion they played a Mozart quartet and the Schubert Quintet, a work that expressed the immense satisfaction which everybody present felt, including the eight ambassadors from the Community, at the forthcoming enlargement of the European family.

Fanfare for Europe opened with a gala night at Covent Garden, a great celebration at which the Queen and other members of the royal family were present. The programme, put together by Patrick Garland and others, was composed of a mixture of music, poetry and drama, drawing on our European heritage. The main musical events, however, were the concerts in the Albert Hall. Among these, one given by Herbert von Karajan and the Berlin Philharmonic Orchestra was particularly memorable. I was delighted that von Karajan had agreed to bring the Berliners for this concert – 'to please you', as he said to me. Their London appearance had to be sandwiched between two long-standing engagements, the whole orchestra flying into London in the afternoon and out again the morning after the concert. Technically the evening was one of the Winter Proms; needless to say, the whole of the Albert Hall was packed, and looking at the mass of young people standing in the promenade it did not seem possible to squeeze another single body in. I shall never forget the faces of the orchestra as they took their places on the platform and found themselves confronted with a typically tumultuous promenaders' welcome. Many of them gave the impression that they were hurriedly looking around for a means of making a quick getaway. Von Karajan himself was visibly stunned by his reception when he came on to conduct Beethoven's Fourth Symphony but, great extrovert that he was, he responded to it and immediately established a rapport with this youthful part of his audience. Afterwards, at supper at No. 10, I learned that he had arrived with a cold, and when I asked him how much rehearsal they had had that afternoon he told me that when the orchestra assembled he had asked them to play a common chord of C and then dismissed them to get a good rest. It certainly worked. That evening produced two superb performances – the Beethoven Fourth and Fifth symphonies. The Fourth has always been a favourite of mine, as has the Eighth. The Fourth, squeezed between the massive structures of the Third and the Fifth, is all too seldom heard, whereas the Eighth, in the same way slotted between the Seventh and Ninth, has always been relatively popular. Toscanini made recordings of the Fourth at different periods of his life, each one getting faster with advancing age. The reverse was the case with Klemperer's performances, which got slower towards the end of his life. I also never expect to hear Beethoven's Fifth played so well as long as I live, and a tape of that night's performance is one of my treasured possessions. No doubt it was the combination of the warmth of the audience and the European significance of the event that inspired von Karajan and the Berlin Philharmonic Orchestra to the very greatest heights of interpretation and technique.

Supper after such occasions with Herbert von Karajan, whether at No. 10 or elsewhere, was always a delight, for we had sailing as well as music in common. This was why, to other guests, our conversation took on something of the nature of a cross-talk. I usually began by asking him about the interpretation of one of the works he had just been conducting; why, for example, had he played a Mozart divertimento in a dry, rather withdrawn way? 'That', he would explain, 'is because I feel that is how Mozart wanted it and that, in fact, is how they did it in his day. Did they tell me', he would go on, 'that you have now got some new and better winches on your boat? How can I get them for mine in the Mediterranean?' Having told him the answer, I might then try to switch back to music again, but all ended amicably with a fairly prolonged session on each of our interests. We never talked about politics. I have known of no more intellectually stimulating person with whom to discuss both the technique and the content of music. After a concert in the Festival Hall in May 1976, at which he and the Berlin Philharmonic Orchestra had given a dramatic and exciting performance of Beethoven's Eighth Symphony followed by such a rich, luscious weaving together in one pattern of all the varying aspects of the hero's life in Richard

Strauss's *'Ein Heldenleben'* as I ever believed possible, I remarked to von Karajan at supper: 'I didn't see you give a single cue to anyone in the orchestra tonight to come in.' 'No,' he said, 'that is not my job. At the concert I look after the structure and movement of the work.' 'You can afford to do that,' I said. 'If someone doesn't come in, he's out – isn't that right?' He laughed. 'Well,' he said, 'they all know when they've got to come in. They don't need me to tell them.'

The opportunities for getting to concerts, opera or ballet whilst I was Prime Minister were limited, but there was some compensation for this in the variety and number of special occasions in which I was able to take part. The last night of *Tristan und Isolde* at Covent Garden on 3 July 1971, with Birgit Nilsson as Isolde, was Georg Solti's last performance there as Musical Director. At a party afterwards in the Crush Bar, I presented him with the Honorary Knighthood of the British Empire, which had been conferred on him by the Queen; Georg is now a British Citizen – and Sir Georg. Congratulating him on his superb performance, I said that I had thought his hold on the last, lingering chord of B major would never cease: the silence was awe-inspiring, so deeply was the audience involved, and it seemed minutes before the applause broke out. He looked surprised. 'I have never before met a prime minister who knew what the chord of B major was, let alone discussed it with me after the last chord of *Tristan und Isolde,*' he commented. Some years later, after dinner at his house, he asked me whether I knew which instrument was missing from that last chord. I had to confess my ignorance. 'Wagner has them all playing until that last chord,' he said, 'but then the cor anglais is missing. And do you know why? Because the cor anglais is concerned with the theme of the love potion, and by the time of the last chord it has done its work. It is no longer needed.'

The following year, in October 1972, I was present in Paris at a con-cert at which Georg Solti celebrated his sixtieth birthday with a concert by l'Orchestre de Paris in the Théâtre des Champs Élysées. It is not often that one goes to a symphony concert on a Saturday morning, but this was a remarkable programme, for after Mozart's Symphony No. 36 came the Berg Violin Concerto and Schoenberg's *Erwartung*. We have become accustomed to the Berg Violin Concerto and to those of Schoenberg's earlier works noted for youthful zestful spirit, but this long piece for soprano and orchestra is both difficult and complex. It gave an interesting insight into Georg Solti's mind, that he should have chosen this for his sixtieth birthday celebration.

My travels as Prime Minister provided many memorable musical experiences. At the Élysée, the presidential palace in Paris, at the din-ner given for me by President Pompidou after our successful negotiations for entry into the Community in May 1971, a string orches-tra played Mozart's *'Eine Kleine Nachtmusik'*, together with some string music by English composers, including Vaughan Williams's arrangement of 'Greensleeves'. In the Emperor's Palace in Tokyo, during my official visit to Japan, the first ever of a British prime minister, the palace mu-sicians played Japanese music on their original instruments dating from around the sixth century. I had already listened to a concert on these instruments at the shrine at Nikko, where I had a chance of talking to the musicians and examining the instruments. The most interesting was a small pipe organ for the mouth, played like a harmonica but with the pipes actually coming up in front of the face in the shape of a pyramid. The other instruments were early types of stringed arrangements on sounding boards and various forms of percussion. The musicians at the shrine regularly meet those at the palace so that the purity of the musical tradition can be maintained free from any local variations.

In recent years, my artistic interests have taken me to Tokyo every autumn, for the ceremonies linked with the Praemium Imperiale arts prizes. The Praemium Imperiale was founded by the Japan Arts Association to take over where the Nobel Prizes leave off. The Nobel Prizes deal overwhelmingly with the sciences – the two exceptions being the Peace Prize and the Prize for Literature – and the Praemium Imperiale seeks to extend the same principles further into the realms of artistic attainment by recognizing and rewarding major international contributions to the arts. I am an international adviser to the committee, which each year selects a winner in five areas and awards them a prize of $100,000. The categories are music; architecture; film and theatre; painting; and sculpture. In the first few years of the prize, many hugely distinguished international figures have already been honoured – including Leonard Bernstein, Mstislav Rostropovich, Sir John Gielgud and the Chilean painter Matta. I find my participation in this committee hugely rewarding and am convinced that the Praemium Imperiale will soon win the international recognition and status that such an ambitious and worthwhile enterprise so evidently deserves.

In Singapore, during the Commonwealth Prime Ministers' Conference in January 1971, I entertained the prime ministers of Australia, New Zealand, Malaysia and Singapore on board HMS *Intrepid*. That evening we had music of a different kind. After dinner, the Royal Marines Band beat Retreat on the flight-deck. Five prime ministers looked down on that colourful scene: the band marching up and down in their white uniforms and topis on the illuminated ship; the floodlight playing on the white ensign fluttering in the evening breeze; the dark Singaporean night blacking out the other ships in the harbour, which had been part of British history for so long, but from which the Royal Navy was soon to depart. The Last Post sounded, the ensign was hauled down; we turned away. There was a manly tear on the face of the Australian Prime Minister.

The Navy always does things splendidly. It made me proud to be able to entertain other prime ministers in such a way. It was not until I returned home that I heard of one of the consequences. My Parliamentary Private Secretary told me that a slight problem had arisen over the cost of the hospitality on board *Intrepid*. 'That was an official occasion,' I told him, 'and should be properly covered as such.' 'That is not the point,' he replied. 'You see, in order to make sure that everything went all right, the Navy had a dress rehearsal of the dinner two nights before, with officers standing in for you and the other prime ministers.' 'Well, that's all right,' I told him. 'It was obviously necessary. We can cover that as well.' 'Yes,' he said, 'but in order to make sure everything was absolutely perfect, the Navy also had exactly the same food and wines as you were going to have. This precisely doubled the bill.' Like everything else with the Navy, a way out was found. It was worth it.

Music was introduced into the celebrations of the twenty-fifth anniversary of the creation of the United Nations, held in New York in October 1970. I was delighted that the Los Angeles Symphony Orchestra was chosen to play on that occasion. One evening, after an official dinner, wishing to get away from all the problems of international politics, I asked my Private Secretary, Robert Armstrong, to nip out and ring up Lenny Bernstein and see if he was at home and, if he was, to come and tell me that there was a very urgent message from Downing Street to which I must attend at once. So he went off and came back explaining about the urgent message, and showed me a piece of paper with nonsense written on it, so I then asked the host of the dinner if he would excuse me as I had to deal with this problem at Downing Street. Then we went out to my car and drove off to see Lenny Bernstein. I wanted to talk about music and he wanted to talk about Vietnam, and we finally finished at two in the morning, when he said that he had to go to the recording studio early that morning to play and conduct Ravel's Piano Concerto. 'I remember you playing that in London with the New York Philharmonic,' I said, 'in 1963.' He ruminated. 'I had forgotten that. What else did I play?' 'The Dvořák No. 2 in D Minor,' I told him, 'and you pulled it this way and pushed it that way until its shape was entirely unrecognizable.' 'Now I remember,' he said. 'God! what a neurotic performance that must have been.'

Somehow my talks with Bernstein always seemed to be late at night. One evening, after the House of Commons rose, I went down to the Albert Hall to watch him listening to the replays of the Verdi Requiem, which he had just finished recording, picking the particular ones he wanted and supervising the mix. All around were technicians, in their shirtsleeves, listening with him to the quadraphonic sound. It was a fascinating experience. On another occasion in my flat in Albany, I pressed him hard on the organization and management of orchestras. At four o'clock in the morning he finally came clean and declared that a firm central authority, be it a conductor or management, was essential if a symphony orchestra was not only to attain the highest standards but, what was even more difficult, maintain them over a sufficient period of time to be in the top three or four of the world class. Bernstein was one of those to whom everything in music appeared to come easily: a brilliant pianist, a successful composer of both musicals and symphonic works, a masterly, if individualistic, conductor, a stimulating writer, and a popularizer of music who could hold any audience spellbound, whether on television or in the concert hall. One cannot but wonder at the extraordinary fount of energy on which he drew – and deplore the manifold attempts to dishonour his memory since his death.

———

At No. 10 we always sang carols round a Christmas tree in the large pillared drawing room. A group from the London Bach Choir came each year to sing to us, as friends and staff all sat around the room, many of them on the floor. On one occasion President Nixon's daughter Tricia and her husband arrived just in time to have a meal and join in. It made them feel at home.

At Chequers we always had carols on Christmas Eve. The carollers came from the local church to sing in the great hall for our Christmas party, with the tree twinkling in the corner and the other lights dimmed. It became quite a tradition and we got to know the choir well. Once, as we were all having mince pies and some wine-cup together, I asked one of the oldest members of the choir whether she could recall this kind of thing ever happening before. 'Yes', she replied, 'but only once under another prime minister. It was when Mr Ramsay MacDonald was here. But then, of course, we had to come in by the kitchen, up the stairs and on to the balcony. We weren't allowed to mix downstairs. Not even Mr MacDonald could fix that in those days.'

Chequers was presented to the British nation in 1919 by Lord Lee of Fareham to provide a country home for rest and relaxation for the British Prime Minister. It is a splendid unspoilt Tudor house containing many treasures, including the State ring of Queen Elizabeth I of England, together with some of Cromwell's letters and Napoleon's letters and papers. What was originally the central courtyard of the Tudor house has been closed in and made into the great hall, which provides an excellent room for concerts of all kinds. There I installed a further set of stereo equipment; there was already a Steinway in the house, but for concert purposes Steinway's always lent us one of their own pianos.

Our first concert at Chequers proved more eventful than we had expected. Isaac Stern, an old friend, suggested that his trio should play a Beethoven programme for me before they started their series of concerts in London. This was arranged for 9 September 1970, during the Parliamentary recess when I hoped nothing could interfere with it. As it happened, the evening came at the height of the crisis over a hijacked aircraft with 300 or more passengers held hostage at Dawson's Field in the Jordanian desert. This also involved Leila Khaled, who had been taken off an Israeli aircraft in London and was being held by the immigration authorities. At least five countries had nationals on board the hijacked aircraft and their representatives were meeting with the International Red Cross at Geneva. Events were moving so fast, and the need for speedy decisions was so great, that it was obvious by the middle of the afternoon that I could not leave No. 10 to go down to Chequers for the concert. When the trio arrived at Chequers they were deeply worried about the possible effects of the crisis on the whole of the Middle East, and they were obviously very tense. I passed a message to them on the telephone, expressing the hope that they would continue with the concert in my absence. Despite all their worries they agreed to do so.

The tension made itself felt in Isaac Stern's playing of Beethoven's Violin Sonata in F, known as the 'Spring' Sonata, but after that it disappeared. This is apparent on the tape recording I have. Rose and Istomin played Beethoven's Cello Sonata No. 3 in A Major, Opus 69, most beautifully. The concert ended with Beethoven's 'Archduke' Trio, because it was known to be my favourite. Isaac Stern said afterwards that as he was playing the Violin Sonata he realized that Beethoven's music was stronger than the anxieties and horror of the political situation: it was at just such a time that one most needed to remind oneself of the values and traditions that Beethoven represented. The other players felt the same and on that eventful night they conveyed it to the friends and neighbours gathered round them in the great hall at Chequers.

Yehudi Menuhin, another old friend, brought some of the children from his school to play at Chequers in November 1970. They were young, but how assured they were. A boy of thirteen was playing the cello brilliantly when he found the pin sliding on the floor soon after he had begun. Yehudi stopped him and we placed a rug underneath his chair so that he could get a proper grip. He was not the least put out and threw off his pyrotechnics with even greater confidence. A pianist and violinist from Singapore brought home to me how much more important a part young people from the Far East are now playing in European music-making, with many others from Japan, Korea, Hong Kong and the Philippines coming on to the scene.

Yehudi himself was not billed to play in the programme, but he had suggested that the evening might conclude with an impromptu performance by the two of us. We had decided to play the Handel Sonata in D Major. I particularly checked with him the edition he used and practised it hard beforehand. We rehearsed the piece together at Chequers before the concert began and all seemed to go well. When the children had finished their part of the concert, ending with the first movement of the Brahms Sextet, I went up to fetch Yehudi from his room. The audience was delighted at the idea of this 'lollipop', but when we began it became obvious, to my astonishment, that Yehudi was extraordinarily nervous. In the second movement he began to play faster and faster, and I had some difficulty in keeping up with him. In the third movement we settled down, but in the last movement we began a race for the finish. Then, suddenly, I had a bad moment: I realized that Yehudi was playing from memory, although he had his music open in front of him, and he was clearly playing from a different edition. Hastily looking to see what had happened, I found that he had jumped four bars ahead of me. I skipped everything to fit in with him and, with a quick adjustment, made sure that we finished together. Our audience appeared to have appreciated the performance; perhaps the slight sense of competition rather than partnership had heightened their enjoyment. Over supper only one music critic commented on the four missing bars.

The pianist Clifford Curzon came down to play at Chequers on Sunday 9 July 1972, my birthday. It was a lovely summer evening. We were able to stroll around the rose garden before the concert and chat outside afterwards. Curzon told me he wanted to play one piece to please himself and one to please me. The first was the Variations on a theme from 'Prometheus' by Beethoven, probably better known to most people as it appears in the last movement of the 'Eroica' Symphony. It is a massive work, seldom played, and one that I would not have thought would appeal particularly to Curzon, but he produced an invigorating, indeed exciting, performance, which he later recorded. After the break, he began to play me Schubert's 'Posthumous' Sonata in B Flat, surely one of the loveliest piano sonatas ever written. Pianists seem to despise Schubert's piano sonatas today, not realizing that many of them require a simplicity, clarity and sureness of technique to express without effort their underlying emotion, which is available only to the very best. I first heard this sonata played by Richter at the Aldeburgh

Festival one glorious June Sunday afternoon. It was pure joy. He played the first movement more slowly than anyone else I have ever heard, and with the repeats it journeyed on effortlessly and apparently endlessly; I never wanted it to stop. Clifford Curzon knew how I felt about it, and that night we settled back to bask anew in the freshness of what was almost Schubert's last great piano work. This work too Clifford Curzon later recorded. Four years later, at an impromptu supper party, at my publisher's house in Paris, near the university, Paul Badura-Skoda, who has recorded all the Schubert piano sonatas, asked me what he should play. 'The B Flat "Posthumous",' I replied, 'with all the repeats.' 'With *all* the repeats?' he asked, somewhat incredulously. 'Yes,' I said, '*all* the repeats.' He sat down at the piano and when he got to the repeat halfway through the first movement, and played the first time bars before going back to the beginning, his wife turned to me in astonishment and said: 'I have never heard those eight bars played before.' It was all part of Schubert's heavenly length. Before this, we had been listening to and applauding some Schumann – *'Papillons'* – brilliantly played by a young Cypriot pianist, Cyprien Katsaris. At the end of the Schubert no one moved. It was so deeply satisfying that no one felt the need to applaud. We rested content.

The Greek pianist Gina Bachauer, who had heard Clifford Curzon's concert at Chequers, said she would like to play for my next birthday concert on 8 July 1973. It was once again a fine evening with the sun shining and the roses in full bloom. After Gina had finished, we once again had an impromptu item – this time unknown to me. Georg Solti announced that he had brought with him a new and important recording, which he wished to play on my stereo before we broke up for supper. Everyone was intrigued to know what this might be. Some of us knew that he was busy doing Mozart's *Così fan tutte* for Decca and we were all delighted when his distinguished singers burst into the sextet *'Alla bella Despinetta'* from the first act of *Così*. The point only became clear, however, when the cast, led by Lorengar, Berganza, Krause and Davies, each in their own language, and then the full company in English, sang 'Happy Birthday, Dear Ted' to the background of a harpsichord – happy birthday greetings indeed. The disc given to me afterwards bears the inscription 'Soldecca Group – Very advanced recording', with the names of the artists followed by the very modest 'accompanist G. Solti'.

Twenty-three years later, at a dinner celebrating my eightieth birthday in the Dorchester Suite of the Savoy Hotel, there was a pause in the middle of the speeches. The compère, the excellent James Naughtie, announced that 'the world's greatest cellist is with us ... Slava Rostropovich is here ... And I wish we had time for the complete Bach Suites.' Slava bowed at his table to loud applause. 'One of the reasons why he is not going to walk on to the platform with his instrument is that of course it might lead to loud popular demands for a performance, say of the B Flat Trio, and Denis Healey would insist on playing the piano ... The maestro says he will not speak, but yesterday he toddled up to Abbey Road on his own volition. He recorded something which I haven't heard and no one else in this room has heard. He says it is the Seventh Bach Suite. I think we can hear it now ...' announced the voice of the *Today* programme. We then heard a hilarious rendition of 'Happy Birthday, Dear Edward' from Slava, accompanying himself on the cello. Once again, music had taken me full circle!

The visit of Dr Caetano, the Portuguese Prime Minister, to London in

July 1973, to mark the 600th anniversary of the first Anglo-Portuguese Treaty of Alliance, gave me the opportunity of commissioning a special piece of music in honour of the occasion, to be performed at my dinner for the visiting Prime Minister in the Painted Hall at Greenwich. I invited Sir Arthur Bliss, the Master of the Queen's Music, to compose a piece to be sung by the Martin Neary singers. For the words, Tom Bridges, grandson of the former Poet Laureate and one of my private secretaries, suggested an English translation of a Portuguese poem, *'Mar Português'* – 'Portuguese Sea', a subject that naturally appealed to me. Sir John Betjeman, the Poet Laureate, was invited to write the English words, and Alan Goodison of the Foreign Office was asked to translate the Portuguese into English to enable him to do so. In order to give Sir Arthur an idea of what was involved, the translation was sent to him before Sir John's poem was ready; in fact, when the Poet Laureate's verses arrived, the Master of the Queen's Music found that he preferred Alan Goodison's translation for the purpose of a musical setting. In the event, we printed both Sir John Betjeman's poem and Alan Goodison's translation in the menu, together with the Portuguese original. Sir Arthur Bliss's music has since been published. It was sung in the Painted Hall by the augmented body of singers under Martin Neary, divided into two groups, one on each side at the top of the staircase leading into the hall, whose resonance greatly helped the performance. It is a splendid piece, to my mind amongst the most effective of Arthur Bliss's smaller choral works. It was certainly a piece for an occasion, and it added lustre to this one.

The concert that will be longest remembered of all those we had in Downing Street and at Chequers will be one I gave at No. 10 to celebrate Sir William Walton's seventieth birthday on 29 March 1972. I felt that, despite the honours conferred upon him, William Walton had not always received the recognition he deserved, in particular from his fellow musicians. This was an opportunity to do homage to him, in which many of his contemporaries could take part. I decided to mark the evening by having some new pieces composed in his honour, as well as by arranging a performance of some of his own work.

The veteran English composer Herbert Howells contributed a grace, the words written specially for the occasion by Robert Armstrong, my Principal Private Secretary. After its first performance at this dinner, the words were adapted to general use, and the grace was published and sung before every subsequent dinner at No. 10. Arthur Bliss wrote a witty piece to some amusing words by the poet Paul Dehn, a close friend and past collaborator with Walton, entitled 'An Ode for William Walton'. This, together with Walton's 'Set Me as a Seal upon Thine Heart', one of the latest of his small choral pieces, was sung by the Martin Neary singers. Then, as we sat round the great horseshoe table, the London Sinfonietta, conducted by David Atherton and with Alvar Liddell as narrator, performed ten movements from *Façade,* the precocious music to words by Edith Sitwell that first made Walton famous. It was a sparkling performance, which brought back all the glitter, the fun and at the same time the hardness of the twenties.

After that, we moved into the large pillared drawing room. As midnight approached, I recalled to everyone there how I heard William Walton asked, in an interview on his sixtieth birthday, whether there was any piece of music he would have liked to have composed himself. Without pausing for a moment, he had replied, 'Yes, Schubert's B Flat Trio.' And so, at midnight, with the Queen Mother and the Waltons sitting on the sofa, and the rest of us – including the Blisses, Herbert

Howells and Ben Britten of the older generation; Malcolm Arnold and Richard Rodney Bennett of the younger composers; Lionel Tertis, the greatest of viola players, then well over ninety, with his wife; the Soltis, Fred Ashton from the ballet, Laurence Olivier, Bryan Forbes, Nanette Newman and those whom many would term the 'Arts Establishment' – Lord Clark, Arnold Goodman, Jenny Lee and the Droghedas, with many other friends – sitting around on the floor, we heard John Georgiadis and Douglas Cummings, the leader of the London Symphony Orchestra and the first cellist, together with the pianist John Lill, play the Schubert B Flat Trio. They had never played it before; in fact, they had never until then played together as a trio. But they had spent the whole of the previous weekend working on it, and they had recognized the first requisite for playing Schubert, to let him speak for himself. The performance that evening had a wonderful spontaneity and freshness about it. It recalled to my mind the days when Thibaud, Casals and Cortot, probably the most famous trio of all time, had often played it together. It was a joyful ending to a happy evening in tribute to an original and distinguished British musician.

When I came to celebrate my eightieth birthday in July 1996 there was, perhaps inevitably, a musical theme to most of the celebrations. But one event in particular brought back memories of my time at Downing Street. The Prime Minister and Mrs Major hosted a birthday dinner at 10 Downing Street in my honour, with Her Majesty The Queen and Prince Philip as the guests of honour. This occasion was a reunion both for many of my Cabinet colleagues from 1970–4 and for most of my closest musical friends: Mstislav Rostropovich, the world's greatest cellist; Yehudi Menuhin, now also eighty years old, and his wife; my dear friend Moura Lympany, who turned eighty a few weeks after me; the wonderful pianist Ivo Pogorelich; and Susana Walton, William's widow, who was as full of vitality and joy as ever. The dinner began with that special grace composed for 10 Downing Street by Herbert Howells to the words of Robert Armstrong, who was also present — sung by a group of singers once again conducted by Martin Neary. I felt as though I had come home and the years had turned back. At the end of the evening Her Majesty told me that she could not ever recall enjoying herself so much. It was certainly a magical occasion.

—

Our last concert at Chequers while I was Prime Minister proved to be even more eventful than our first. Isaac Stern and Pinchas Zukerman were both coming to play a programme of violin duos on 27 October, the same programme that they were giving at the Royal Festival Hall two days later. Alas, earlier in October, the Yom Kippur War broke out and brought tensions between the Israeli and British governments. Pinchas Zukerman felt unable to play but Isaac Stern, for the sake of his friendship with me, and even though it might expose him to criticism, decided to take part. The programme had to be completely changed, but it led to the most momentous musical evening we ever had. As the Amadeus Quartet were coming as guests to Chequers, I invited them to bring their instruments with them, and they opened the concert by playing the Haydn Quartet, Opus 54 No. 2, which they had been play-ing at the Edinburgh Festival the previous month. Isaac Stern brought down with him a videotape of Pablo Casals's last ever performance, in Tel Aviv. After Stern had described the occasion, we showed this video-tape on the screen in the great hall. It was intensely moving to watch and hear the frail Casals playing with the utmost simplicity a little piece called 'The Nightingale' for unaccompanied cello. It was a lovely message to leave with the world. The atmosphere was very emotional when Isaac Stern began to play Bach's Chaconne in D Minor as his own personal tribute to Casals, whom he had known so well. He had not been playing for very long when the hairs of his bow broke and he had to interrupt his playing to fetch another bow. He came back shortly afterwards, made a brief apology, and then gave an unforgettable performance of the Chaconne. My private office subsequently recovered the hairs from the broken bow, had them set in transparent plastic and presented them to me as a Christmas present. This concert showed once again how music can triumph over the conflicts and indeed the agonies of mankind.

CHAPTER FIVE

CONDUCTING
AT HOME

——

There can hardly be a musician anywhere in the world who has not
wanted to conduct a well-known symphony orchestra, who has
not sat in the audience and felt his fingers moving as they itched to wield
the baton, or who has not looked up from his chair in the orchestra and
thought how much better he could do it than the fellow on the podium.
If only the conductor could be just a little indisposed – nothing serious
of course, just enough to prevent him going on to the platform – he
himself might step into the gap. The orchestra would respond, the audience would be impressed by his assurance, the critics would acclaim
him, long-sought recognition would be at hand; his future would be
bright. And, after all, it has happened; not very often, but often enough
to keep alive every young musician's dream; it was how Toscanini found
himself one night taking charge of the performance instead of being on
a cellist's desk. No doubt he would have broken through at some time
or other, but he seized his opportunity and became probably the world's
best-known conductor. Leonard Bernstein's break came when Bruno
Walter contracted influenza.

It had always been my dream, ever since I had begun to conduct a
mixed-voice choir in my home town of Broadstairs when I was fifteen.
As an organ scholar at Oxford I had done my share of conducting with

choir and orchestra and once a year since then, at every Christmastide, I had conducted the Town Carol Concert at my home. As my political profile increased, these concerts had become well known through their coverage on radio and television, and had given much pleasure to people beyond our locality. The transition from this to conducting a professional symphony orchestra was a considerable – and daunting – one, but how could I resist when André Previn, the principal conductor of the London Symphony Orchestra, invited me on their behalf to conduct a piece at their Gala Concert on 25th November 1971? Having at once accepted the invitation, I had to decide on the piece to play.

I chose Elgar's 'Cockaigne' Overture for a number of special reasons. It is a bravura piece, which shows off every aspect of the orchestra in its vivid depiction of London as Elgar conceived it. But, by the same token, this Overture can quickly reveal any weakness in an orchestra, either in the individual players or in the quality of the ensemble. Elgar himself was always punctilious in specifying every detail that he required in the orchestral playing, and to observe these meticulously is demanding enough; but the Overture has many changing themes to represent the ever-changing pattern of London life, and these themes are so closely woven into one fabric, that without the greatest understanding among the players, and between them and the conductor, the work can fall apart at the seams.

'Cockaigne' was, in fact, the first bravura piece with orchestration of such brilliance to be written in England. It was also first performed by the London Symphony Orchestra – another reason for my selecting it. Elgar himself made two recordings of the work, one in 1926 with the Royal Albert Hall Orchestra, the other in 1933, towards the end of his life, with the BBC Orchestra. It is extraordinary how these two recordings differ. It is well known that composers are very often not the best conductors of their own works, because of their difficulty in conveying to the orchestra their real intentions. But for anyone who believes that the composer does nevertheless secure an authentic version of his composition, these two recordings will come as something of a revelation. It is also true, though perhaps somewhat surprising, that there are the usual little difficulties in both versions. After coming off the pause in the third bar, for instance, there is a mad scramble by the strings to try to get back to the beat, and again the strings don't quite get the turn after the trill before swinging into the theme for the last time – but what is really so striking is the difference in presentation of the whole work in the two versions.

So I chose 'Cockaigne' above all because it is an ideal gala piece, and because it is a depiction of London – but also because, in 1963, I had heard the New York Philharmonic Orchestra under Leonard Bernstein play 'Cockaigne' at the Festival Hall as the last item in their programme. Never before had I heard it played so brilliantly and with so much panache. It wasn't only that the orchestra was in tremendous form or that the work suited Bernstein's style superbly well; what I felt was that I was hearing it played by people who really believed in themselves and in what they were playing. They had the same attitude that we in Britain had had when the work was written at the beginning of the century, and their 'Cockaigne' contrasted strikingly with the rather lifeless, ironed-out versions to which we had become accustomed. That night I felt that we needed to have the kind of faith in ourselves that this vigorous, buoyant American interpretation seemed to embody. As Prime Minister, I wanted the British to regain their former pride and ebullience, not through empty pomp and circumstance but through the knowledge that deep down they were capable of coping with the challenges of a changed, and continuously changing, world. Perhaps the right performance of 'Cockaigne' could convey something of that.

Only a month earlier, the House of Commons had voted decisively for UK entry into the European Community. The works of Elgar are deeply entwined in our relationship with the European mainland; although he is often seen as a quintessentially English composer, it was in Germany that several of Elgar's most important works first took root. This is particularly true of the First Symphony and the 'Enigma' Variations.

Fitting in orchestral rehearsals is no easy task for a serving Prime Minister: the first rehearsal was the day before the performance, and the second was on the day itself. Handling a rehearsal is far from easy. Nothing is more important for the conductor than to know precisely what he wants in the performance of a work and exactly how he proposes to get it. Ideally, the rehearsal should lead to a work being so well prepared that at the performance the orchestra plays its way through the work without the conductor having to keep adjusting everything as he goes along. What a fallacy it is to think that the man up there on the podium, always busily ssshing here and shouting there, is really doing an effective job as conductor: that ought to have been done long before. All too often on the night it is a mark of under-rehearsal or over-fussiness – or both. But to reach the ideal state I have described – and the few really great performances I have heard in my life have been like that – it is essential to be able to organize the rehearsal properly and to make the fullest use of the always limited time available. The conductor must know clearly in his mind what he wants to obtain from it and how he intends to apportion the time he has been allotted. When the Hungarian-born conductor George Szell achieved the highest technical standards with the Cleveland Symphony Orchestra, his remarkable successes were attributed to the fact that he 'even rehearsed the inspiration'. That is precisely what a conductor should do.

I have always believed in explaining my conception of a work to the choir or orchestra at the beginning of a rehearsal, and I did so on this occasion. I suspect that the orchestra was gently taken aback at what may at first have appeared to be presumptuous and unsolicited advice to the group on whom Elgar himself had relied. But I had a purpose. I wanted to conjure up in their minds the imagery Elgar was trying to convey. I wanted to get that extra bit of bounce into the Londoner in the opening bars. I wanted that extra richness in the luscious, flowing tune conveying the confident splendour of Edwardian London. I wanted that extra touch of gentleness for the lovers as they strolled through the park and into the church. I wanted the horns to think of themselves as an organ when they played the soft reflective music there; an organ with the swell pedal gently opening and closing but without changing the smooth passage of the music. And just before the band arrived, I wanted no ordinary up-and-down scales on the strings but the real bustle and excitement of a crowd as they jostled on the pavement, craning their necks and pushing their neighbours forward in their attempts to see the guardsmen as they came into view; above all, I wanted the great swelling tune to lead to a climax such as there had never been before.

When I first rehearsed the LSO, I was allocated an hour to deal with a piece lasting eighteen minutes. I knew that time was precious, and we wasted none. I had to work hard at individual passages that evening because I knew that the time allocated to me for rehearsal the following morning, the day of the concert, was very short. Above all, I had to pay constant attention to the balance of the orchestra. This always brings immense difficulties because the conductor is at the centre of the sound, whether it be the softest murmur he can cajole or the wildest furore he can control, and yet he has to achieve a balance that will be maintained throughout the concert hall. Nowhere is this more testing than in the Festival Hall in London. It is always described as 'dry' – in other words, lacking in resonance. A real degree of resonance gives richness to orchestral sound; it can at the same time hide many a mistake. No orchestra can afford to take the Festival Hall for granted, least of all one used to playing under resonant conditions, for here every single line of music is clearly audible and balance becomes all the more important. The utmost precision and the most careful balance between instruments are required.

Back in the early seventies, the London Symphony Orchestra was an unusually young band, and one well used to the Royal Festival Hall. My main problem that evening was to convey to them what I wanted. I knew what I wanted – the problem was how to get it. Was I overawed by such a task? Looking back on it, yes. Perhaps that made me rather stiff and wooden; my conducting at that first rehearsal was quite unlike the relaxed, adaptable style I had always cultivated. Nevertheless, I went home well content, feeling that we had made good progress.

The rehearsal the next morning was at ten o'clock. In theory I had only been allocated a quarter of an hour, less than the length of the overture itself. The previous evening I had gone through the score again and made a note of the points where I still felt I had not got it quite right. I started by telling the orchestra about these specific problems and then proceeded to rehearse each in turn. It was only then that I had a final rehearsal of the complete work. This, of course, was reversing the order of the previous evening. The complete run-through went extremely well, so well in fact that I wondered if it could go as well on the night. André Previn then took over to rehearse the rest of the concert and I went back to No. 10 to get on with my day's work.

First there was a meeting of the Cabinet, over which I presided. Starting at eleven o'clock, it lasted until 1.15 p.m. Then, after a quick lunch, I had a meeting with my private secretaries about the questions I had to answer in the House of Commons that afternoon. At three o'clock I went across to the House and dealt with questions, both those of which notice had been given and all the supplementaries that followed. I then had to sit and listen through the first part of a debate on Northern Ireland, after which I went back to No. 10 for some other meetings. It was seven o'clock before I could go up to my flat to change into a white tie ready to go to the Festival Hall. 'Quite a day's programme, one way and another,' I thought to myself as I was getting ready. 'Quite a contrast, too, with other conductors, who could go off for a rest and a sleep between their final rehearsal and the concert!' No matter, there had been no time to worry about further details in the score, or whether everything would go as planned. It had been an extraordinary day, in fact, but then not often does a prime minister in office carry out such an extraordinary assignment as conducting one of the world's great symphony orchestras in a gala concert.

In the Festival Hall they had allocated me a 'green room' to myself. There for some time I sat in solitary state. It seemed at first that everyone thought that before a concert the occupant should be left alone. However, things gradually began to happen. The orchestra librarian came to collect my score to put on the stand. I asked him to see that it was at the height I had measured that morning, and with the right tilt. Isaac Stern, who was playing the Sibelius Violin Concerto in the concert, put his head round the door to enquire how I was. While we were chatting, André Previn appeared to tell me that he was going on first to introduce me; afterwards, the concert manager appeared to say he would give me the cues when to leave my room and to go on the stage.

By this time it was almost eight o'clock and everyone suddenly disappeared. Then came the light tap on the door and the concert manager's voice: 'We will now go to the edge of the platform so that you can hear what André says.' Together we sat by the curtain that hid us from the packed hall. 'A lot of money in the house tonight, sir,' said one of the attendants. André Previn went up to the platform to the loud applause that always greets him. His witty remarks did something to relax an audience that was tense with anticipation – or should I say curiosity? – but not at all certain what it was about to see happen. Then I got my cue and went on to join André, happy that all the preliminaries were almost at an end. At this point I really wished we were going to open with the National Anthem, just to relieve some of the nervous tension I felt and which I was sure the orchestra shared. It certainly had that effect when, some years later, I conducted a gala performance of the Bournemouth Symphony Orchestra; but that night we had to go straight into 'Cockaigne'.

The concert was recorded, and EMI issued the record shortly afterwards. It sold all over the world and remained in the catalogues for many years. The first time I played it I suddenly realized how different everything sounded in the concert hall compared with a sitting room. In 1996 EMI remastered their recording of this performance and the improvement was quite startling. Although I would probably change my interpretation in some respects, I am still immensely proud of this performance and I am delighted that it is back in the catalogue.

I had been able to do things in the Festival Hall, in the atmosphere of that Gala Concert with a responsive orchestra and a highly strung audience, that one would never even have thought of doing when recording in a studio. It only goes to show that there is a difference between the real thing and a recording. There was another surprise in store for me, however: when I turned over the record for the rest of the programme, I found that the concert performance had disappeared. When I enquired what had happened, I found that André Previn had taken the LSO off to the EMI studio the following week and had recorded the other works there. They had not had to rely on one performance straight through, deal with the acoustics of the hall or put up with the odd cough in the background. 'André,' I said when I next saw him, 'you've cheated!' And so he had, but I am always glad that my recording is the one taken on that memorable night, with all its flaws. It is a recording of what for me will always remain an exciting occasion.

What I could not realize at that time was that, twenty-five years on, I would have conducted so many of the world's finest orchestras in a wide range of repertoire. My conducting schedule is still extremely busy, and I have enjoyed immensely the opportunity to share my love of music so directly with audiences right across the world.

I conducted the LSO again when they celebrated their seventieth birthday, in 1974. I had the privilege of conducting Wagner's Overture to *Die Meistersinger,* which had been the first item in the orchestra's first ever concert programme – conducted by Richter.

A symphony orchestra has a life of its own. More than a hundred people constantly rehearsing together, playing together and for a large part of the time travelling together, often for quite long periods abroad, get to know each other's whims and idiosyncrasies well. It is on tour that the humorist emerges, keeping the rest entertained and relaxing the tension when things go wrong; at the same time, those who like to keep themselves to themselves quietly disappear into the background.

In May 1975 I travelled with the LSO to conduct 'Cockaigne' in Bonn and in the famous Gürzenich Hall in Cologne. The orchestra had its own special plane; the fun, the ragging, the badinage on board were tremendous. André Previn, the LSO's permanent conductor, was in the midst of this; not for him the splendid isolation maintained by some conductors in an attempt to uphold their status. He was one of the boys and enjoyed it. At the rehearsal in Cologne the atmosphere was far different; there was an immediate concentration on the work in hand, not from a desire to get through the whole programme but from a need to test the hall and then to polish up those bits of the works where difficulties had previously been encountered.

This particular tour lasted only three days, but after it I was better able to imagine the effects of one lasting three weeks or more; the continuous strain of constant travel, the upsets from eating strange food, the complications of working in a fresh hall each night and the tedium of playing the same programme, or a variant of it, at each concert. Yet these orchestral tours, which have increased so much over the last forty years, are of immense importance for the listener. The opportunity of hearing great orchestras from other countries enriches our musical lives. My regret is that orchestras – or individual musicians for that matter – so seldom have the opportunity of listening to one another. What could they not learn from such an experience?

At a lunch in Bonn at which many of my musical, political and sailing friends were present, a journalist approached André. He was not a music critic, he explained, but he wanted to give the LSO a good general write-up because of the immense impact it was making on this tour. One thing, however, was worrying him; perhaps André could help with an explanation. 'Of course, if I can,' answered André. 'I am told,' said the journalist, 'that when you are conducting, both you and Mr Heath use a score. What is the explanation of that?' 'Oh, that's simple,' replied André, 'you see both Mr Heath and I have perfectly good eyesight.' This answer obviously baffled the journalist and André, taking mercy on him, added: 'You see, conducting without a score became fashionable after Toscanini. His eyesight was so poor that he could not read one on the podium. Ever since then many people have thought that to be a great conductor you need to do without a score. It's not really relevant: it's the result that matters.'

I have no doubt that those who can master and memorize a score completely have, on the whole, an advantage over others when conducting an orchestra. On the other hand, if part of their mental energy is devoted to remembering the score, rather than concentrating on what the orchestra is doing, it seems to me that they are at a partial disadvantage. Equally so is the conductor who has to have his head buried in the score the whole time. But the use of a score should never be held against any conductor; it can certainly be of help to have one at hand when anything goes wrong. It is the conductor who can handle a complete opera without a score who is taking the greatest risks, not only with the orchestra but with singers and chorus; perhaps he is most to be admired when he pulls it off. I once watched Karajan conduct a performance of *Die Meistersinger* at Salzburg – lasting four hours – without a score. When I went to see him in his room before the last act, he was refreshing his mind from the score, 'but only the structure, not the details', he said. It was that emphasis on the structure, that complete

134

confidence in the orchestra, singers and chorus playing their part, that enabled him to produce such a magnificent performance.

André Previn's reply to the press correspondent notwithstanding, I have seen him conduct on many occasions without a score. He himself recalls some of the hazards, however. On one American tour, the LSO were playing Beethoven's Fifth Symphony and Brahms's Fourth Symphony as two of the major items in their programme, reversing the order on alternate evenings to make some slight change and thus relieve the tedium of the tour. One night, towards the end of their visit, André waved the librarian aside, saying: 'Don't bother to put the score on tonight – I'll do without it.' He went on to the stage fully convinced they were beginning with Brahms's Fourth. After the applause that greeted him he turned to the orchestra and lifted both hands high above his head, ready to bring in the drooping phrases of the opening bars. Just as he was poised for this moving moment, he heard the leader of the orchestra say clearly and firmly: 'Beethoven Five.' All he could do was drop both hands to his sides and reposition himself for the very different entry required for the opening notes of Beethoven's best-known symphony. But he had been saved.

Incidentally, I find the opening bar of Beethoven's Fifth the most controversial of any orchestral piece, though I seldom hear it discussed amongst conductors. The normal practice is to emphasize its three quavers equally, with a tendency for the main emphasis to come automatically on the first. Two bars later, however, as soon as individual instruments begin to play the same phrase in the way in which it is valued in a complete bar, the emphasis naturally comes on the second of the quavers. The contrast between the second version and the first, coming so quickly after the opening bar, is so marked that I find it jars.

Moreover, it is difficult to justify intellectually. I have yet to hear the performance, however, in which a conductor tries to reconcile the two.

After André's narrow escape with Beethoven and Brahms, he asked some of the section leaders, as they travelled to the next concert on a special plane, whether they minded him conducting from memory. 'No, Maestro,' one replied, 'so long as you remember it,' adding significantly, 'but if by any chance you don't, let *us* put it right.' That was very wise advice to any conductor from an old hand. What the conductor does when a soloist has a momentary lapse of memory is a more difficult question, which fortunately I have never had to answer in practice. Every conductor prays it may never happen!

In a chamber orchestra the musicians can hear each other playing and much more easily co-ordinate their phrasing, while the conductor, with a glance or a slight movement of a hand, can bring out whatever he wants in the way of emphasis or light and shade. This was first brought home to me when I conducted the English Chamber Orchestra at the concluding concert of the Windsor Festival in October 1975. The entire evening was devoted to Mozart, starting with the lively and amusing overture to *The Escape from the Seraglio* and with the Symphony No. 29 in A Major as the concluding item. This is an enchanting work, which I have known for many years and about which I have very clear ideas. It is easy to produce a humdrum performance, for left to itself the music will play itself; but to give it elegance and to bring out the natural feeling that the young Mozart put into it is a more difficult matter, which requires detailed rehearsal. We rehearsed from 11 a.m. to 2 p.m. on the day and again from 3 p.m. to 6 p.m., with the concert at 8 p.m.: a strenuous day. At the morning rehearsal, after running through and polishing the *Seraglio* Overture, I concentrated on the Symphony. Over a cup of coffee during the first break, I asked one of the young violin players how he thought it was going. 'Very well,' he replied, 'but I wish you would give up your LSO habits.' 'What do you mean by that?' I asked him, to which he replied: 'Well, I can quite understand that when you are up there with the LSO and three thousand people in the Festival Hall you need to use that long beat and all that energy, but here with us you only need to raise an eyebrow or a finger and we will give you what you want at once.' It was a salutary lesson, which I took to heart. On the other hand, there was also something in that rehearsal for the orchestra, and when we had finished more than two hours' hard work, one of the section leaders said to me: 'You know, we must have played Mozart twenty-nine dozens of times, but this is the first occasion for years that we have been made to go through it section by section, and at times bar by bar, to get exactly what the conductor wanted.' Normally, without sufficient time for rehearsal, it is difficult for a conductor to secure the reading he has clearly in his heart and mind; he has to make do with the conventional, with as much of his own superimposed upon it as can be managed.

After the Overture, Gina Bachauer played Mozart's Piano Concerto in C Minor. Accompanying a soloist, whether a singer or instrumentalist, on the piano or with an orchestra, is an art in itself. It demands a degree of understanding and a readiness of response from the pianist or conductor which is quite different from the individual, personal reading that is the norm for them. Accompanying Gina Bachauer was a remarkable experience. Our overall concept of this Concerto was the same; it is a work in a big mould, the shape of which is set by the orchestra in its lengthy opening introduction on the theme that is later taken up by the piano. It is therefore essential that the orchestra's phrasing of the introduction should be fashioned in the same way as the pianist's later on. The reverse is the case in the quiet, simple slow movement where the piano opens with a delicious tune – which can in itself be phrased in a variety of ways – which the woodwind and the orchestra then emulate. Gina Bachauer's phrasing was so clear that it was a joy to precede or follow her. At the same time, on points of detail she knew exactly what she wanted and we were able to respond accordingly.

After the Concerto and before the Symphony I included the motet 'Exsultate, Jubilate' for soprano solo, which finishes with a glorious burst of praise on the word 'Alleluia' to one of Mozart's finest tunes. I had got to know this when I was organ scholar at Balliol and I had always wanted to accompany it. It is a testing piece, and to achieve Mozart's purpose the 'Alleluia' requires a high soprano voice, which can throw off the aria with the greatest freedom, including a joyous top C in the last 'Alleluia'. The young soprano Felicity Lott, now a Dame and still delighting audiences all over the world, did just this. Some people said to me when I planned this programme that a whole evening of Mozart might turn out to be rather monotonous in content. Nothing could have been further from the truth. The contrast between the wit of the *Seraglio* Overture, the emotional depths of the C Minor Piano Concerto, the joyful outpourings of the 'Exsultate, Jubilate', and, finally, the tunefulness and spontaneity of the A Major Symphony, produced a programme which not only showed many different aspects of Mozart's creative personality but was also deeply satisfying. I was delighted when, after the concert, people came up to me to say that they were going away feeling happier than when they had arrived.

More and more is being done in Britain today to enable young people to appreciate music at an early age. For over fifty years the concerts started by Sir Robert Mayer provided children with an opportunity of hearing short, individual works for orchestra and soloists, preceded by an explanation of what the work was about. There is now a nationwide organization, Youth and Music, which opens up the entire world of concerts, operas and live theatre to anyone under thirty years of age with the good fortune to be one of its subscribers. Like those young people's concerts, Youth and Music owes its existence to the late Sir Robert Mayer.

I conducted the fiftieth anniversary concert in that Robert Mayer series at the Royal Festival Hall at Christmas 1973, a time of year that gave me the chance of including carols in the programme. Accustomed as I was to leading an audience in this sort of concert, it was a fascinating experience to conduct 3,000 children in the Festival Hall and to find out how readily they responded to my request for bold singing, good phrasing and clear diction.

Rossini's Overture to his opera *Cenerentola* – 'Cinderella' – was an obvious piece with which to open a Christmas concert for children. It was appropriate that the orchestra was the BBC Academy, now sadly defunct, which consisted of young musicians training as orchestral players before embarking on a professional career. 'Tom Sawyer's Saturday' by John Dankworth needed no introduction: Mark Twain's words, narrated by Richard Baker, spoke for themselves. As a piece for narrator and orchestra, it is of the same genre as Prokofiev's 'Peter and the Wolf', but in his music Dankworth shows more of the syncopated influence of modern jazz. I also included in the programme one of Handel's organ concerti, No. 4 in A. These concerti are all tuneful works, many of the tunes having been pillaged by Handel from his other compositions. Perhaps the best known is that in B Flat, with an opening much akin to

the Alleluia Chorus from the *Messiah*. The Fourth Concerto has long
been a favourite of mine and I tried to explain to the children the dia-
logue between the organ and the orchestra in terms of boy meeting girl
and what happened thereafter, a simple 'word picture' – many others
might equally well have been contrived – which held their attention
because it related their own experience as young people to the music.

A word picture of this kind can also often be helpful to those playing
instruments in an orchestra, as I found when rehearsing another of the
items in this concert, 'The Entrance of the Queen of Sheba' from
Handel's *Solomon,* a work for strings, two oboes and bassoons in which
the oboes have a prominent and difficult part to play. But to me the
strings are not just playing semi-quavers one after another, they are sim-
ulating the crowd rushing to the vantage points, jostling one another in
their eagerness to see the arrival of the Queen, while the oboes are not
just oboes playing in thirds together – they are the heralds of the advancing procession. Thought of in this way, this little piece takes on an added
attractiveness for younger players as well as listeners.

Most of this concert was restored to the record catalogue by EMI
along with the 'Cockaigne' from the 1971 LSO concert, and a performance of Johannes Brahms's 'Academic Festival Overture' in which I
conducted the European Community Youth Orchestra in Aberdeen in
August 1978.

—

Conducting has given me the opportunity to perform with several outstanding soloists.

I have played with Moura Lympany a number of times, and she is still
a dear friend of mine. We have done the 'Emperor' Concerto twice, once
with the Bournemouth Symphony Orchestra at the Newbury Festival,

and once in France. I first met Moura in the mid-sixties. She used to come to my flat in Albany where we would discuss and play music together for hours on end.

Moura was responsible for establishing the festival at Rasiguères, which I attended on several occasions. As there was no proper concert hall, the concerts were held in the wine cellars below the hall where we would eat our meals. The 'hall' seated only about 250 people and the stage was tiny as well. The Manchester Camerata came down and performed for us. They were on holiday and were not paid for their performances. However, their accommodation and entertainment were gladly and enthusiastically provided by the local townsfolk. The festival had a very intimate setting. Moura gave several excellent recitals and various other artists also performed. Time was almost irrelevant during such a festival. Concerts that were scheduled for 8 p.m. would often begin sometime around 9 p.m. and dinners planned for 10 p.m. would not start until after midnight. Sadly, the festival ceased to exist a few years ago due to financial problems.

Moura also participated when I accepted an invitation to conduct the Bournemouth Symphony Orchestra at a gala concert in October 1975 in order to raise funds to establish a new concert hall, rehearsal hall, library and administrative centre. Not only was the orchestra known for its young and enthusiastic membership, but I felt personally indebted to Bournemouth music. As a boy, on holiday with an aunt and uncle near Southampton Water, I had often cycled through the New Forest to Bournemouth to hear Sir Dan Godfrey conduct the Bournemouth Municipal Orchestra at his Wednesday afternoon concerts. I recall particularly one brilliant performance of Rimsky-Korsakov's *Scheherazade* after which I cycled all the way home for a very late supper.

At the 1975 concert I conducted the first half of the programme, which consisted of Beethoven's Eighth Symphony followed by César Franck's Symphonic Variations for Piano and Orchestra – a lovely work now seldom played – with Moura as the soloist. She brought out all its romantic characteristics and delighted the audience with the scintillating, rippling finale. The orchestra too enjoyed the concert; one of the youngest members said, as he watched the audience leaving in their dinner jackets and long dresses for the gala Champagne supper: 'It's the first time I've seen an audience properly dressed and worthy of the orchestra.' An orchestra cares just as much about its audience as the audience does about the performance.

As a contribution towards raising funds for the fiftieth anniversary of the Battle of Britain, I agreed to conduct a concert for the RAF in Canterbury Cathedral in 1990. This had been my local cathedral for the greater part of my life, being the one nearest to my home in Broadstairs. I used to go every year to sing in the festival in Canterbury, also in that glorious cathedral, which still has immense appeal. The concert was once again played by the Bournemouth Symphony Orchestra, which I have known ever since the early thirties and conducted fifteen years earlier. Given my own long-term association with the Bournemouth Orchestra, I was particularly delighted that they were going to come to Canterbury. We opened the programme with Beethoven's 'Leonore' Overture No. 3, which I had also recently conducted in Salisbury Cathedral, where they were concerned about having the solo trumpet high in the cathedral. Canterbury had no such problems.

Moura played Mozart's Piano Concerto No. 21 in C Major, of which she is particularly fond, and she moved it along beautifully. Very calm and controlled, she was in her element, and got a great reception. After the interval we played Dvořák's 'New World' Symphony – very appropriate for the anniversary of the Battle of Britain, with which we had set about trying to create a new world.

I have conducted many soloists who are excellent, but difficult to follow – in particular, Pogorelich, Rostropovich and Nigel Kennedy. But one must have an instinct of what they are going to do, which comes from knowing them well. If you work closely with them, it becomes almost automatic, and I think that Ivo Pogorelich would agree with that. I have conducted him in performances of the Chopin Second Piano Concerto twice in Salisbury Cathedral – and his interpretation of the second movement is wonderfully free, but terribly difficult to follow. We therefore needed an orchestra that would follow us, for if the orchestra tries to go its own way it is hopeless. In July 1996 the English Chamber Orchestra showed how a really fine orchestra can triumph in this situation.

I first met Ivo a number of years ago when he was requesting British citizenship. We met several times whilst I helped him to become a citizen, and during this process I got to know him quite well. He likes to live in England, but he hardly ever performs here. I remember well when he was competing for the Chopin Prize. At the competition, the Russian judge was instructed that under no circumstances would Ivo receive any points at all. When the rest of the panel discovered this, half of them walked off. Now, everybody remembers that it was Ivo who did not win the prize that year, but hardly anybody remembers who did. I heard one concert with Pogorelich in the Festival Hall when he performed César Franck's *Symphonic Variations,* after which he was much criticized for only giving the audience twenty minutes of music. Well, it was not his fault that Franck had only written twenty minutes!

I think my eightieth birthday concerts made up a good series. The first one was in Oxford in the Sheldonian Theatre, where I conducted Elgar's 'Serenade for Strings' and Schubert's Fifth Symphony.

The second concert was in Wiesbaden. They had just started the Rheinland Festival, and the pianist, Justus Frantz, had inaugurated it. He asked me if I would go over and join them. He wanted to do the Mozart Piano Concerto K488, and had an orchestra that had just been founded for the festival and which is intended to be permanent. It reminded me how festivals differ between countries. When I got there for the rehearsal, the courtyard was packed with people, there were beer stands all over, and I was warmly greeted. Everyone crowded round, and as we went in to the hall, all these people followed us in for the rehearsal. After the Mozart, Justus said that he was going to finish by doing Schubert's Symphony No. 9, and I said: 'My God, are you going to play all the repeats?' He replied: 'Oh, I hadn't thought about that. What do you think?' I said that since it was almost eleven o'clock, if he were to play all the repeats, then it would be after midnight by the close of the concert. So he agreed that perhaps he ought not to play all the repeats. But then, in the concert, he just went on and on and on. That is quite different from the attitude that we have at British festivals, for we are always so stiff and formal, with everybody on their best behaviour.

I have conducted in Salisbury Cathedral four times and they have been very special occasions for me, especially since they have contributed to the upkeep of the cathedral and the spire. They were also special in the works I performed and the artists who were playing them. The last occasion was my third birthday concert of 1996, and the cathedral was really packed. We were able to have Ivo Pogorelich playing the Chopin

Piano Concerto No. 2, in a way in which only he can play it. Afterwards we had a discussion as to whether it was the way Chopin would have played it, or whether it was entirely Pogorelich, but nobody could call into question Ivo's breathtaking technical brilliance. Then we had the Bruckner *Te Deum,* a splendid work and very suitable for the cathedral. Bruckner himself thought that it was the greatest work he ever wrote, and at the end it has the glorious theme from the Adagio of the Seventh Symphony. Furthermore, the opening string figure is the same as that from Bruckner's sketch of his Finale to the Ninth Symphony. The piece was first performed under the baton of Gustav Mahler, who praised the work for 'the majesty of its architecture and the nobility of its ideas'. He also changed his own copy of the full score, writing in place of 'for soli, chorus, organ and orchestra' that the work was for 'the tongues of heaven-blessed angels, for seekers of God, for tormented hearts and for souls purified by flames'. Given the right performance, that is no overstatement.

At times it is possible to criticize Bruckner for being too repetitive, but I think that this comes from his training as a church organist. The great pauses that some of today's conductors put between Bruckner's phrases are unwarranted, but his music does have a great majesty about it and enormous contrasts, and there is so much that conductors can do. I heard a recording that Muti did of the Fourth Symphony – that is the first of his symphonies that I got to know well at Oxford – and I thought initially that it was a good recording. But I thought I should remind myself of other examples by playing the Furtwängler recording, which was done in about 1948 and has now been put on CD. When I put it on, it was like hearing a completely different piece of music, and Furtwängler had in those opening bars a shimmer that Muti had never even thought of. Herbert von Karajan too has done some excellent recordings of Bruckner, much better than his ones of Mahler.

Salisbury Cathedral has given me the opportunity to produce works on a large scale. It is not always necessary to play religious music there, but you must be careful, because there is some secular music that comes off badly when juxtaposed with the full glory of the cathedral. On such occasions we have managed to fill the cathedral with more people than attend most other events held there. The cathedral itself has a large amount of resonance, of which a conductor must be aware at all times, as well as a slightly sharp organ. But the majesty of the setting is more than ample compensation. Furthermore, it has the advantage of being able to accommodate over 1,500 people, all of whom can hear well, and most of whom have a good view.

My fourth birthday concert was at Kenwood, and it was the best evening I have ever known there. I conducted Weber's Overture to *Oberon,* then I did Delius's 'Summer Night on the River'. I greatly prefer his 'Walk in the Paradise Garden', but someone else had already fitted it into a programme later that month, so I chose the former. Then we did Schubert's Fifth Symphony, and used Handel's *Water Music* as the finale and encore. Justus Frantz was supposed to be there that night to play the Mozart, but he did not arrive, so we were running around trying to find him. We then discovered that he had not boarded his plane from Germany. So we searched for a new pianist, and found Angela Hewitt. However, since we found her so late, we were forced to play it with only a short rehearsal, and the English Chamber Orchestra was very flexible and put in some extra time to ensure that it would work. Playing from the music, she gave a performance that was both refined and gripping. Playing in the open air at any time produces problems.

Will the sound reach the audience sitting on the grass? Will the orchestra blend properly? Will the instruments, which normally carry in a concert hall, carry in the open air? At Kenwood they used to have an amplification system that was less than satisfactory, but now they have a new system that produces splendid results. I don't know whether the lake in front the the orchestra is there to prevent deranged fans from getting at the orchestra, or whether it is to provide a depressed conductor with the opportunity to immolate himself after a bad performance. Either way, it makes a glorious setting. The 11,000 people there that night seemed to enjoy themselves just as much as I did.

Then there was the concert with the BBC Concert Orchestra in the Hippodrome in Golders Green, a wonderful old theatre that has been converted into a recording studio. This began with the young American researcher in my office, Christopher Joyce, playing a Britten piece for solo trumpet. We shared the programme with a number of people. I did the first movement of Schubert's Fifth Symphony, then I conducted a piece entitled 'Morning Cloud', which was originally written for me and the Black Dyke Mills Band by Robert Farnon, but was then brilliantly reorchestrated for symphony orchestra by Pete Moore. Then there was the Brahms Academic Festival Overture. I once heard this piece done in Germany, and they made a horrible mess of it. I said to them: 'But these are your tunes!', but they were still hopeless. The BBC Concert Orchestra eventually took to it after some rehearsing. Then we did the slow movement from the Beethoven Triple Concerto, a beautiful and moving excerpt from a great but underrated concerto, which I have always loved. Unfortunately, the movement ends on a dominant chord, and we could not have that, so we rewrote Beethoven. Then we had Delius's 'Walk in the Paradise Garden', and we ended with Elgar's

'Cockaigne' Overture. As a surprise to me, the head of my private office, Michael McManus, then came on and conducted Aaron Copland's arrangement of 'Happy Birthday' to end the concert. Denis Healey and David Jacobs were the two commentators, and the entire concert was broadcast on Radio 2 later that week. Denis Vaughan, formerly Sir Thomas Beecham's right-hand man, conducted other short works and my dear friend Rosemary Squires sang some songs for me. The audience on that night included two ambassadors — and I hope that they, and everyone at home, caught some of the joy of the occasion.

CHAPTER SIX

CONDUCTING
TRAVELS

——

I was involved in founding the European Community Youth Orchestra and in the early days I conducted the opening item at its concerts. It was formed because we wanted to show that there was more to the European Community than simply fruit and vegetables and arguments about tariffs. We believed that Europe and its history amounted to much more than this; and we could show through music that this was the case.

Three of us in London worked out how we would get an orchestra formed, and then we had to raise the money. We persuaded the EC to finance it in part and then we had to deal with each government in turn, and they all agreed to put up some money. Then we had to work out how to select the players, how they would play together as an orchestra, and how we would arrange concerts and tours. This took a number of years and we finally resolved it in 1977.

For the first tour, we had the initial rehearsals in England and the first concert in Amsterdam. Then we toured all the capitals. The hall in Amsterdam is magnificent, and we were able to rehearse there, but I had an argument with the permanent conductor, Claudio Abbado. I had sent invitations to the concerts to all the heads of government and royal families and, since they would all be there, felt that we must have the appropriate national anthem at each performance, and also the European anthem. Abbado declared that we were not going to have any anthems, and I replied that in that case we were not going to get any royal families; so he told me that if I wanted national anthems, then I would have to conduct them. I said: 'Very well, I will do that.'

So in Amsterdam we had the Dutch national anthem and the European anthem. At the end of the rehearsal, after the Wagner Overture, I went on to the anthems. On Sunday evenings during the war, the BBC used to play anthems and the more Allies we got, the longer this took. So I had a slight recollection of the Dutch national anthem. When we played it through, the leader of the orchestra, who was a young Dutchman and turned out to be a very good leader, said that my tempo was too slow; the leader of the cellos, however, who was also a young Dutchman, said it was too fast. So I stuck to the speed I had just taken. At that moment I noticed someone behind me on the podium, so I turned and there was a very tall, lean Dutchman. He asked if I would mind playing the anthem through twice at the concert itself. I said that if he knew the trouble I had in playing it through once, he would not ask such a thing, and enquired why. He replied that the Queen would come from her private room at the top of the balcony, down the stairs and along to the front of the hall and that it would take her precisely two national anthems' worth to get there. So we agreed that I would play the anthem through twice before the European national anthem.

Before we played, I told the orchestra that there must be no pause between the national anthem and the European anthem – we must go straight on. As it turned out, however, after we played the national anthem there was an enormous burst of applause and we could not proceed. I learned afterwards that this occurred because we played it with such enthusiasm and gusto, which they had never before encountered in the Netherlands. When the tumult died down, I went on with the European anthem, at which point there was the noise of 3,200 seats being lowered as everybody sat down – but that was only the beginning. Afterwards we learned that the Queen turned at this point to the chairman of the youth orchestra and said: 'What is this? I thought it was supposed to be the *Meistersinger* Overture?' To which the chairman replied: 'No, ma'am, this is the European anthem.' The Queen then said: 'If this is an anthem, then shouldn't we be standing?' To which he answered: 'Well, it is customary, ma'am.' 'Very well,' she concluded, 'we will stand.' So halfway through the anthem there was the noise of 3,200 seats being pushed back again as everybody stood up. That was our first experience of the new world of protocol which our orchestra would open up.

The next incident occurred in Paris: while we were rehearsing there, another tall figure appeared and said that we were not allowed to play the national anthems that night, because the French had had an election and the President had not yet nominated a new government. So I said: 'Very well, then go off to the Elysée and tell the President that I am conducting this concert tonight and I wish to play the *"Marseillaise"* and the European anthem.' The visitor looked rather grim but went away. Later he came back and said that the President would announce the formation of his government at 7.30 p.m. and I might play the two national anthems at 8 p.m. It turned out that many of the drums were manned by young Frenchman, so when I proposed the *'Marseillaise'*, they all threw their sticks in the air in delight but warned me that the President had recently changed the speed of the *'Marseillaise'* because, he said, when it was written it was meant to be a slow march. I replied that we didn't want a slow march, we wanted a quick march, and the young men threw their sticks in the air again and we then rehearsed it with great fervour. That evening the new Prime Minister of France came to the performance. When we burst into the *'Marseillaise'* there was a mass of booing; and when it stopped, we burst into the European anthem and there was a mass of cheering. Afterwards there was another enormous cheer. At the interval I asked the Prime Minister what had gone wrong with the *'Marseillaise'*, and had I taken it too fast? He said: 'No, it had absolutely nothing whatsoever to do with you. It was because I was there in the central box, and when you played the *"Marseillaise"*, everybody looked at me and booed. When you played the European anthem, they were so delighted to have Europe that they cheered, and they were cheering you and not me.'

—

I have worked with many young players, in particular with the Academy of the BBC, and they are very willing and prepared to do anything, and if you want extra time they do not mind in the least. But the Academy of the BBC could not compare with the resources that the ECYO had to choose from. Most of the EC countries have a very high standard in the conservatories from which musicians are drawn. In the beginning, Germany was reluctant to join the ECYO, because they thought it would steal people away from their existing youth orchestras. We also discovered that the British were more comprehensive than other countries, because we always had full brass, full percussion and a full string section, which many of the other countries did not.

This was particularly true of the Italians, who felt very strongly about this, and that they were rather inferior. When we had a concert in Milan in 1978, we had a press conference at which the press raised this issue with me. I said that it was entirely up to the Italians how they educated their young people, but if they did not have them playing brass, then we could not have Italians playing brass in the orchestra.

By then we had arranged that there would be two independent musicians present at each of the auditions, so that we could make sure that the same levels of performance were being maintained throughout the audition process. When this process was complete, sometime before Christmas, they came to me and said that the net result was that there were 126 people for the orchestra and 66 of them were British. I said that we could not really have more than half of the orchestra British. We needed many of them in the brass and percussion sections, which other countries could not always staff in strength, but managed to adjust the total down to thirty-three British members, which was still a high proportion.

For rehearsals we used to have eighteen days before we started the tour: eighteen days in the French Alps. The youngsters enjoyed this, as they were able to swim and play tennis with each other as well as rehearse. They did a lot of free rehearsing on their own when something needed polishing. Unfortunately, Abbado tried to fool about with them and they used to try to fool about with him, and would all change their parts in a piece, which was meant in good spirit, but was really just a waste of time and did not do much for the quality of the performance. They did, however, also work quite hard. Some of them went on to form what is arguably one of the finest chamber orchestras, the Chamber Orchestra of Europe. This does not give opportunities to new musicians in the same manner as the ECYO, because we laid down from the outset that when musicians reached the age of twenty-two they had to leave us. So we always experienced new influxes of musicians.

I invited von Karajan to conduct the ECYO in Salzburg and he said:

'No, but you can bring them to Salzburg and play, and I will see what they are like.' After hearing them he agreed that I could bring them the following year and he would conduct them. This was arranged and I duly sent him the programme we were doing, and he refused it all. He wanted to do the Beethoven Violin Concerto with Anne Sophie Mutter and Mozart's Symphony No. 41. Typically, von Karajan arrived with us by helicopter down the slope of the mountain, and he was tremendous during the rehearsal; and Anne Sophie Mutter was phenomenal. After he had done his two pieces, he asked me to hold the orchestra there, as there were two things he wanted to do. First, he asked the first violin if he could sit in his seat. Then von Karajan said: 'Now, when I come on to the platform, you stand. We will now rehearse that.' So he gave the chair back to the violinist. Then he said: 'I am in. Stand. You can't behave like droopy, half-dead people. I said "Stand" and that is what we will now rehearse again.' He repeated this three times before they finally got it right. Then he said: 'When we are finished, it is the audience's job to applaud. You as the orchestra don't applaud yourselves, and you don't applaud me. It is the job of the audience to do that, do you understand?' That evening all went well, the orchestra stood and looked very smart. After the Mozart, the fifth time that von Karajan came back on, a young cellist began stamping his feet, just as Abbado got them to do. Von Karajan got level with him and then his elbow went right into the fellow's ribs, and he stopped stamping his feet.

—

Around 1976, I began to receive an increasing number of invitations to conduct orchestras all over the world. I was delighted when Georg Solti rang up and asked if I would like to do a whole concert with the Chicago Symphony Orchestra. This differed from most of my previous conducting engagements, as I would be the featured guest conductor for the whole evening with one of the finest orchestras in the world.

When I arrived in Chicago we had only one rehearsal, in the morning, and we were told that we had to finish at 12.30 p.m., by which time I had just got to the last three pages of Elgar's 'Enigma' Variations. The orchestra had not got it right at the very end, so I said that we would go back a bit to get it absolutely correct. Then I had a feeling that there was someone standing behind me and I turned round and there was another of those very tall, lean men, who told me that I had seventy-two seconds. I said I needed to go back and do one more part, and he simply replied that I now had fifty-five seconds. I was furious, so I slammed the score shut and told the orchestra that they would just have to be all right that evening, and walked off. They did get it right that night. The hall was packed and I did a Wagner overture, Beethoven's Eighth Symphony and the Elgar. It was a gala concert, and all the money went to the Musicians' Pension Fund. Afterwards I was invited to the house on Lakeside where a post-concert party was being held. When I got there the Chairman of the Trust greeted me and then a Mr Hemphill rushed up and heaped all sorts of praise on me for the concert. I said: 'Thank you, I am glad you enjoyed it.' He replied that it had nothing to do with enjoyment: he was an honorary trustee of the orchestra and had agreed to underwrite that particular concert. For once he did not have to produce a dime, which was absolutely wonderful!

Some time later the Chicago Symphony Orchestra came to the Proms and although Georg Solti got through the concert magnificently, he was not at all well. I went to the reception afterwards, when Solti came up to me in the lift and said that I had to protect him, for he could not stand much more of the reception. I ushered him to a table in the corner and

—

then drew up a chair, which blocked everything, and sat down on it. Then a man came up whom I recognized as the thin stranger who had stood behind me when I was rehearsing the orchestra on that previous occasion. He explained something to Solti, who replied that it was his own fault, because his watch was a little slow, and he apologized for going over his time. The thin man said that, since Solti had apologized, it was all right. I asked Georg if he had gone over his rehearsal time, and he said that he had, by a minute and a half. I thought I was the only one they treated like that, but I was wrong – they treat everyone like that!

Eugene Ormandy invited me to conduct the Philadelphia Orchestra soon after that in 1976, and I did so on the 200th anniversary of the United States, which I was delighted to do. I conducted the 'Cockaigne', and Ormandy was highly complimentary, presenting me with a beautiful bowl, which has stood in pride of place in my house ever since. The only problem in the 'Cockaigne' rehearsals came before the last episode, where the work slows down after the twist in the theme. In the rehearsal it was difficult, but that night it went very well and everybody was delighted. I found Ormandy to be a very enjoyable personality and we got on well together.

He also gave me a recording of a fascinating Toscanini rehearsal of the Overture to *The Italian Girl in Algiers* by Rossini. After the orchestra starts playing, Toscanini says: 'Stop, bad, no good, start again.' They start again, then he says: 'Bad, no good, not it, start again this way.' They start again and he screams: 'Idiots, idiots, idiots, why not play proper, once more.' They start again, and they stop as you hear him break his baton, and he throws it on the ground and says: 'I go away, I come not back, idiots.' Then you hear him go off. There is a pause, then you hear him say: 'I come back, play again.'

The trend has moved away from the standard dictatorial conductor, but I don't think that a democratic orchestra can really succeed. I think it is just a way for the orchestra to feel that they do not have to meet the requirements of the conductor, as they used to in the old days. I believe that whether or not the members of the orchestra agree with them, conductors are there to produce a work, and the musicians must do what the conductors want. Orchestras are not meant to be democratic manifestations, they are meant to produce music. You want the orchestra to have trust in you, and if they see that you are going about it in the right way, then they will trust you.

Orchestras can change from time to time in their standards. I think Chicago is still at the top; the New York Philharmonic and Cleveland are moving upwards; the Philadelphia Orchestra is roughly the same. I do not hear much about the Boston Symphony. The foreign orchestras I have conducted have always been very responsive to me. I have conducted some of the university orchestras in the United States and they have done very well. They are extremely anxious to please when they have a foreigner conducting.

I had known Lorin Maazel for a long time when in 1978 he invited me to conduct part of a concert in the summer festival of the Cleveland Orchestra. They use the superb Blossom musical centre, about thirty miles outside Cleveland in a very good country setting, with excellent facilities. I gladly accepted and we agreed on the programme. I would conduct the Brahms Academic Festival Overture, but before that I would be the narrator in Copland's *Lincoln Portrait*. In the rehearsal, we started with the Brahms and I was surprised at how much time was available. Lorin Maazel was at great pains to emphasize that I could have as much time as I wanted to rehearse the orchestra really thoroughly – a luxury which a roving conductor can rarely, if ever, enjoy. Copland's *Lincoln Portrait* certainly is a remarkable work. I got into difficulties with some of the pronunciation, but found the whole experience thoroughly enjoyable. We had some 11,000 people in the semi-open hall that night, and I cannot help but envy orchestras that have such superb facilities at their command.

—

While von Karajan was with the Berlin Philharmonic, I had a standing invitation to conduct them. I wanted Isaac Stern to join me and play the Beethoven Concerto with them. He experienced great difficulties over this, because his wife's family had suffered under the Nazis and he would never play in Berlin. I tried to influence him and say that he could not go through life like this for ever. I thought he had to make a reconciliation, just as others had made reconciliations. Menuhin did so and was much criticized at the time, but that has all now been accepted. Stern said that he would like to, but he simply could not.

This went on until the early eighties, when there was a concert to celebrate Robert Mayer's 100th birthday, and Yehudi and Isaac played the Bach Double Concerto. I could not go, as there was an election campaign under way and I had to go and speak in the Midlands. But the next morning Isaac called me up and asked if he could come to lunch. I said that I would be delighted, then he rang again and asked if he could bring Artur Rubinstein, to which I acceded. Then the office rang up and said that Rubinstein wanted to bring his girlfriend with him. So again I said yes, of course. Stage by stage the housekeeper became more desperate. Isaac arrived early for lunch. He asked whether I was still interested in him playing in Berlin. 'Of course,' I said. But apparently he had tried again but had failed to convince his wife that he should do so. So I said that was too bad. Then Rubinstein and his girlfriend arrived, so we had drinks and then lunch. During lunch, Isaac addressed Rubinstein and said: 'Ted is trying to persuade me to go to Berlin and try to make things up. What do you think about it?' To my astonishment, after a long pause Rubinstein replied: 'Yes, you should go and you ought to go now.' This flabbergasted Isaac, who stopped in his tracks and did not resume the conversation.

Later Isaac asked the time and, when told it was a quarter to three, said that he must leave at once. He explained that he was off to Tokyo, and then on to give a concert in Beijing. So he got up and dashed for the door, but I persuaded him to stay and have some cognac. Rubinstein later told me that Isaac had told some white lies about the concert of Bach's Double Concerto. Isaac had said that it was a wonderful evening and that he and Yehudi had played it successfully, but Rubinstein said that although Isaac and Yehudi had played well, they were two different men, playing two different concerti in two different times.

The first time I met Rubinstein was after a marvellous concert in London in the 1960s. Afterwards we had supper with some friends at their home, near Buckingham Palace, and the host asked Artur if he would like some port or brandy. Artur said that he was playing another concert in twenty-four hours' time and so could not have anything to drink. Somebody asked if this had always been the case, and he replied that it had, ever since he was fifteen. Apparently, he was playing a concert in Paris and it was the first big concert at which he performed. At the rehearsal that morning, nothing would go right and he felt very depressed. The fellow who had set the concert up said that Artur should not be depressed, but should come and have some lunch. So off they went to a very nice restaurant where he ordered champagne. So the young pianist drank some champagne, and rather liked it. So he drank some more champagne, and then they had lunch and his host ordered claret. So Artur drank some claret and rather liked it, so he drank some more claret. In the middle of the afternoon they finished lunch and Rubinstein went back to the place where he was staying and sat down to practise a little more on his dummy keyboard. Nothing would happen – his fingers would not work – and he was terrified and did not know what to do about it. He rang the landlady who told him that he must drink a lot of coffee. Then he went to the bathroom, turned on the cold tap and had a cold bath until he could stand it no longer, drank some more coffee, then went back to the cold bath. He did this for some two hours until his fingers began to work again and he could play the concert, but he swore never again to drink before a performance.

I never ended up in Berlin conducting Isaac Stern, but my opportunity to conduct the Berlin Philharmonic came in 1978, when the orchestra was performing a long concert in Paris, mainly for broadcast on television and radio, and in instalments. Herbert von Karajan asked me to do the 'Cockaigne', and we had rehearsals the day before and on the day of the concert. The orchestra had not played it before and we had to work quite hard at it. That night at the reception the leader came up to me and said: 'Well done, but you know to do that, the orchestra had to do a lot of hard work.' They had recognized that – something no British orchestra would ever admit to.

In the summer of 1985 I went on a ten-day trip to Turkey. This was mainly a political visit, but I got time to take a break and conduct the Istanbul Philharmonic, which I was delighted to do. It was a charity concert, the orchestra played well, and we got a very warm welcome.

Earlier in that year I had done two concerts in Israel. Before accepting

Reciting Copland's Lincoln Portrait: *'Fellow citizens, we cannot escape history ...'*

LEFT: Presenting a cello to David Willcocks at the Royal College of Music.

BELOW: With David Oistrakh.

ABOVE: The early days of the European Community Youth Orchestra.

BELOW: With Felix Schmidt, cellist.

ABOVE: Conducting the blind musicians of Beijing.

BELOW: The pleasure and the pain ...

Recording the Beethoven Triple Concerto with the Trio Zingara — Elizabeth Layton, Felix Schmidt and Annette Cole; also present is Sabih Shukri, sponsor of the recording and a good friend of the Arts.

Above: With Angela Hewitt, pianist, Kenwood Bowl, July 1996.

Left above: My eightieth birthday concert with the Oxford Orchestra da Camera, Sheldonian Theatre, May 1996.

Left below: Visiting the Majors at Downing Street with Slava Rostropovich, July 1996.

Rehearsing the inspiration!

the invitation to conduct there, I consulted several other people who had conducted the orchestra in Jerusalem and they all said very good things about it, so I accepted. The first concert was in a kibbutz. When we arrived, we were shown all round the kibbutz and saw the homes in which the kibbutzniks lived. I was very concerned about their lifestyle, for they hardly ever left the kibbutz until they were nineteen years old. I wondered about this different way of life, to which very few of us in the West can relate. Anyway they made an excellent audience, and were only bettered by the one in Jerusalem, where we got a tremendous response to Dvořák's Ninth Symphony. The Israelis were very interested in my interpretation and afterwards while we were having drinks there were some enthusiasts arguing about whether I had taken the Largo of the 'New World' too fast – they just wanted to have it played very slowly so that they could soak it all up. Perhaps they had been listening to Leonard Bernstein!

—

I had arranged to go to China in the spring of 1987, starting in Shanghai and then going on to Beijing. I received an invitation from the symphony orchestra in Shanghai to conduct them in a concert on a Saturday evening, and they invited me to choose a programme. As soon as the Beijing Orchestra heard about this, they asked if I would conduct in the Great Hall of the People – and they wanted their concert to take place before the Shanghai concert. I replied that this was not possible, as I had undertaken first to go to Shanghai, and fortunately Beijing accepted this. Shanghai then came back and said that there was so much interest that they wanted me to do two concerts, with the first now on the Friday, which I accepted. Then came a further request to do a concert on the preceding night too, the Thursday, and I accepted that as well.

When I got to Shanghai, they asked if I would do a fourth concert on the Saturday afternoon and I replied that I could not do more than three concerts. We then started rehearsing at the beginning of the week. The hall was old and not very satisfactory. The Shanghai Orchestra, however, is the oldest in the People's Republic of China, established in the thirties, and they were very enthusiastic and obliging, although there were certain weaknesses in the brass. The programme I chose consisted of Wagner's *Meistersinger* Overture, Edward Elgar's Serenade for Strings and Borodin's Polovtsian Dances from *Prince Igor* in the first half; Dvořák's 'New World' Symphony completed the evening.

After the first hour and a half of the initial rehearsal I stopped and said: 'Now is the time for a break.' Everything I had said up to that point had been interpreted by the first violinist, who spoke perfect English. He looked at me and said that he was puzzled, and I asked him why. 'I don't understand what you mean by "It is time for a break,"' he replied. I said that we were halfway through the rehearsal, and now was the time for all of us to have a rest. He still looked puzzled, but interpreted this to the orchestra; then he came back and said that the orchestra did not understand why this was necessary. I replied that my union, the conductors' union, insisted that I have a rest halfway through the rehearsal, and that I would now go to my room and have some orange juice and a rest, so he should tell the orchestra they could do whatever they liked, so long as they were back within quarter of an hour. Then I left the platform.

On the second day, halfway through the rehearsal, I said to the first violinist: 'Kindly tell the orchestra that my union says that I must now have a break.' He interpreted, then replied that the musicians' union said that that was a matter for mutual discussion, to be settled by agreement.

I said: 'The musicians' union? You didn't have one yesterday.' 'No,' he replied, 'but after you told us about your union, we met before the rehearsal this morning and formed the musicians' union. So we must now agree about having a break.'

The three concerts were packed, and the orchestra played better and better as the evenings wore on. Both orchestra and audiences liked the programme. The Elgar Serenade got a particularly loud burst of applause that was sustained for some time. And the Chinese of course approved of Dvořák's 'New World' Symphony, which is loved everywhere.

I then moved on to Beijing, where a number of friends had decided that this concert should set an example by raising funds for charitable purposes. We decided that the money should go to a children's charity and that children suffering from deafness should be provided with a new home, with full medical facilities. Two former members of my staff now based in the Far East did a tremendous job contacting firms from the United States and Europe to raise funds. The net result was that we raised something in the order of $250,000. The home was duly built and I visited it three years later with the disabled son of Deng Xiaoping, Deng Pufang, who had taken a particular interest in the project.

The Great Hall of the People accommodates 8,000 people and that night it was packed full. I was told that everyone of note was present, except Deng Xiaoping himself, who told me that because he suffered from deafness in one ear, he thought the seat would be wasted, which I quite understood. I saw him after the concert and he said that, because of the length of the programme, it had been necessary to delay the evening news bulletin on all radio programmes throughout China. This was the first time it had ever been delayed for anyone, but he had ordered it out of respect for me and my concert.

The Beijing programme consisted of Elgar's 'Cockaigne', Tchaikovsky's Variations on a Rococo Theme and Dvořák's Symphony No. 9. Felix Schmidt played the Tchaikovsky. When asked the reason for choosing Dvořák's Ninth, I said that in the West we had made a mess of the old world, and now we were looking to the People's Republic of China to play a leading part in creating the new world. Before I went I received a message from the Chinese, asking if I would do some Chinese music, and I said that I was quite keen to do so if they would give me the orchestral score well in advance. They replied that there was no orchestral score, only a piano part, and that the orchestra consisted entirely of Asian instruments played by musicians who were totally blind. That was a rather alarming prospect, but the musicians had a remarkable unity in their playing and I gave them the introduction on the piano. They then took over, and they played well and the Chinese audience was absolutely delighted.

I went off to the western provinces right after the concert, and whenever I walked into a hotel or along the street, people stopped and pointed at me and said: 'The music man.' They had all been watching the concert on television that night, and it was calculated that some 400 million people had seen it.

The Chinese musicians played extremely well, especially the strings. I think that in the next century the Chinese will produce many of the world's great cellists and violinists. They already have a remarkable number who are leading soloists across the world, and we in the West might not keep up with them. It is not the same in the brass or piano, however.

There was an interesting difference that I found between orchestral playing in China and that of Japan. When a new hall in Tokyo was opened, there were five opening concerts. The first four were meant to be conducted by von Karajan with the Berlin Philharmonic, but he was taken ill, so they were conducted by a Japanese conductor. I was invited to conduct the fifth concert, given by the young musicians' orchestra, strengthened by professionals. The leading cellist from Berlin played the Haydn Cello Concerto in D Major as part of our concert, and he was extremely good. Afterwards he told me that he regarded me as one of the true classical conductors of these concerti.

The concert hall in Tokyo is superb, but the seating looks odd because it is so varied. The acoustics are admirable, and the whole design was obviously very carefully planned. The day after the concert I took part in a discussion with artists of various kinds, representatives from music and painting, and so on. I was asked about my view of the Japanese symphony orchestra now that I had conducted one. I replied that what had interested me was the contrast between the Chinese and Japanese orchestras. The Japanese had players of a uniform, very high quality. When you rehearsed them, they became more and more unified, and they remained at the level they had reached at the end of the last rehearsal. The Chinese were not of such high quality, perhaps because of the effects of the Revolution, but they were much more flexible. If you were conducting a Japanese concert and tried to introduce a new element into the performance, because you happened to be feeling joyous and exhilarated, or possessed by deeper, darker emotions, you could not do so; no matter what you did, the musicians would still produce the performance of the last rehearsal. But if you tried to do that with the Chinese, they would respond. Perhaps they would not be as effective technically, but they would respond to the emotion you were trying to put across. This I think has remained the case – the Japanese are excellent, but rigid; the Chinese are less good, but flexible.

One of my Balliol contemporaries and a great friend, Dr Wallace Brookes became Dean of the University Medical School in Salt Lake City, and from time to time when I was in the States I would stop off there to visit him. I then received an invitation from the Mormon hierarchy to conduct part of a symphony concert there in 1990. I agreed to do this and it was a tremendous evening, marking the fiftieth anniversary of the Utah Symphony Orchestra. I opened the concert with Dvořák's Carnival Overture and they suggested the Vaughan Williams violin piece, 'The Lark Ascending', to be played by the permanent conductor and one-time leader of the orchestra, Joseph Silverstein. I have always enjoyed this piece, from the time I heard it performed in Canterbury Cathedral in the early thirties. What I had not previously realized was that if you have the conductor of an orchestra taking the part of the soloist in a concerto, he has an almost irresistible temptation to conduct the orchestra at the same time. I fully recognize that the job of a conductor is to accompany and accommodate the soloist, but the clash of wills on this occasion was rather great, although the audience seemed to like it. The orchestra too was not of the same quality as the great American orchestras, although it seemed to be well funded, judging by the high standards of their hospitality. The evening raised a huge amount of money for them.

In February 1991 I went to the Soviet Union to conduct a concert in St Petersburg. I agonized over the choice of music for that night and finally decided that I wanted to perform Bruckner's *Te Deum*. I wondered how a Communist nation would respond to the *Te Deum,* but when I discovered that near by there resided an excellent chorus that had originated in pre-Communist Russia, I simply had to try it. That night I also did the Tchaikovsky Variations on a Rococo Theme with Felix Schmidt. After the concert, a number of us went to a large ship, which was said to have a good restaurant. When we arrived, they told us that the restaurant had closed, but they would be happy to serve us dinner in the ballroom, which was still open. We gladly accepted and were led into a large ballroom, where there was a stale-sounding dance band but nobody dancing. Midway through our dinner I commented that the problem was that the band was too dead and that we ought to heat it up. When they finished one particularly dreary piece, I strolled over the the band leader and asked him if he had the 'Tiger Rag'. He said that he did, and when they all had their music up, I gently nudged the conductor aside and said that I had better take this one. As we played, people got up and started dancing. They liked it so much we had to play it twice.

—

In the great European and American orchestras you do not have substitutes but have more musicians than the full orchestra needs, because some players rehearse for, and play in, only one half of the programme. However, they will take part in all the rehearsals for their part of the programme and they will not be substituted at any later time. The budgets for foreign orchestras are several times the equivalent figures for British orchestras. For example, the leader of Chicago gets an enormous salary and automatically becomes the chief instructor of the local university. He also gets a very large pension, travelling expenses and clothes, which seems unbelievable to our musicians, because his salary alone is already many times what our people get. They do not one, but five concerts of a programme in Chicago, and the hall is full for each one of them. This is an entirely different basis of operation, and is replicated across the world – in America and Germany most widely.

Behind the success story of musical performance in the United States is a pattern of funding quite unlike what we are used to here in the United Kingdom. There is no national public subsidy in America, and most of the money coming into the arts is privately endowed. In this country most of the private funds of our wealthier citizens are tied up in trusts for the next generation, so people don't use them for investing in the performing arts. You can't do this in America, so people pay their money to an orchestra instead of paying tax on it, as it is tax deductible.

There is also another big difference between US orchestras and their European counterparts – especially those in this country. In the United States, there is a tradition of training orchestras to play like chamber ensembles, with the individual players and sections of the orchestra paying close attention to one another, as well as to their scores and their conductor. The London Symphony Orchestra benefited enormously from being coached this way by Michael Tilson Thomas, and the Anglo-American conductor Richard Stamp and his Academy of London are also achieving some quite remarkable results this way. Another failing in Britain is the fact that we have a huge number of orchestras, but hardly any seem to have a significant number of established permanent members; many of the best orchestral musicians crop up again and again in different bands.

Of our British composers in the last century I think that Elgar and Britten have made the most impact abroad, but music is still in a transitional stage, and nobody knows what is going to come out on top. In autumn 1996, I attended a concert of twentieth-century Chinese music for strings, and I am convinced that this music could win a sizeable popular foothold in the West, combining melodic invention with both energy and inwardness. It is organizations such as the BBC that have continued to promote modernistic works from the nineties in the face of public opinion. If you ask them why they do this, they have not got a real reason, and are embarrassed by it. I cannot help feeling that there is an element of protectionism about the BBC, and I certainly do not believe that conductors and musicians have a responsibility to perform modern works simply because they are new; I think they should perform what they think is good music.

British orchestras are very good at sight-reading and feel that they can perform anything on the spur of the moment, and I do not know anywhere else in the world where an orchestra would take such a view. Other orchestras would say that it is their job to come in and work hard on a piece until it is ready to perform. I know that this is the attitude of the Berliners, and of the New York and Chicago orchestras. This is one reason, in my opinion, why British orchestras never get right to the top and the world never quite believes that a British orchestra is the world's greatest. They will never get down to making sure that everything is as perfect as it can be. To achieve that requires a large number of rehearsals – and if you have got someone organizing matters or getting in a particular conductor, that naturally means much more expense. When I do concerts now, I always stipulate that there must be at least two full rehearsals. The organizers always protest that nobody else asks for that, so why do I want it? I say that I insist on it, in order to attain a proper standard. The second thing I insist on is that the musicians who take part in the first rehearsal must be those who take part in the second rehearsal. I also want a guarantee that the same players will take part in the concert itself. Organizers reluctantly give in, and I like to think that the results prove my point.

Whether they like it or not, whether they know it or not, people do have spiritual needs and it is the arts that can meet them. Music can do this; pictures can do this, the theatre and the ballet can do this, but there are some problems. The great thing about music is that the language is the same for everybody. Music works this way both spiritually and intellectually. Theatre, for example, is not always accessible. Often language gets in the way and there is a need for translation. Once a translation has been done, the nuances of the original frequently disappear. A fully accurate translation is virtually impossible. In opera, similar problems exist, but in the hands of a skilful translator, that hurdle can be overcome – although many will sympathize with the famous words of Sir Edward Appleton, who wrote: 'I do not mind what language an opera is sung in so long as it is in a language I don't understand!' In the best operas, after all, the plots are usually simple to understand, and the finer points are usually well expressed in the music, so that they are easily recognized. People can enjoy ballet, particularly when it is accompanied by accessible music, without an intimate knowledge of its techniques or even the storylines. But many people find it difficult to understand everything that is going on, especially in a typical modern ballet, and many of the finer points are lost. As far as painting is concerned, the period in which an artist paints is so crucial that, in another era, it is often difficult to judge if the artist was successful at what he was attempting. This was a problem that Picasso had during his time, and I believe that it is even more difficult to judge his paintings today than it was when he was painting them. In the end I believe that it is this spiritual need in people that music satisfies so well and which, as I have been lucky enough to discover, can truly be a joy for life.

CHAPTER SEVEN

MUSIC – A JOY FOR LIFE

——

Music is all-pervasive. It permeates almost every aspect of our daily lives. Perhaps the extent to which this is so is not fully recognized because we still speak of those who are interested in music and those who are not; for while there are clearly some who are more interested than others, virtually everyone is continually encountering and responding to music in everyday life. It has become so much a part of us that we accept it for the natural thing it is and take it for granted, without needing to ask ourselves whether we are among those who *do* or those who *do not,* so far as music is concerned.

It used to be said that a few days after a new Verdi opera appeared you could hear the errand boys whistling the tunes in the street. They knew good tunes when they stumbled upon them, but their whistling was not just an act of musical appreciation: in some way it made them feel better and it provided an outlet for their own emotions. Today new operas no longer have that sort of tune and the prevalent trend of popular music is rhythmic rather than melodic, while other factors such as the growth of the recording industry, and the ready availability of broadcast music have produced changes in the ways we encounter and use music. But still the occasions are there when the 'non-musical' can and do actively participate.

The World Cup Final at Wembley in 1966 was one of the most exciting events I have seen in my life. The excruciating tension of extra time
was almost unbearable. How stirring it was to hear the crowd all around
singing 'When the saints go marching in' more and more lustily as the
tension grew. When England beat Germany the pent-up emotion was so
great that there was a lump in most throats. This tune, although simple
as music goes, is a good one, and here it met a deeply felt need to create a bond between spectators and players, to express a common
purpose – support for one's side and the urge to win.

The same is true of marching songs of every army in the world. They
all have the same characteristics of simplicity and unity which can be
used to maintain morale and create pride of purpose. Those we used in
the West in the two World Wars are well known; I have listened to thou-
sands who sang them, reliving their experiences, in the Albert Hall on
the eve of Remembrance Sunday and joining in as lustily as ever they
did, although most of them would be the first to claim that they were
not musical.

So eager have armies been in the past to secure a good tune that they
have sometimes stolen one another's. To many it must seem a bizarre
aspect of the Second World War that troops on both sides of the conflict
should have claimed possession of 'Lili Marlene'. Many of the army songs
I have heard in Beijing are purely Western in idiom and have been handed
down from Mao Zedong's 'Long March', although several were added
later to reinforce the ideological position of the Chinese People's Army.
The approach may be different, for the British in particular often use
humour as a weapon, but in purpose there is not much to choose
between 'We'll hang out the washing on the Siegfried Line', with which
the British defied Hitler, and 'We'll take Tiger Mountain by our strata-

gem' – it sounds better in Chinese – to which Chairman Mao's soldiers marched.

But to come to more solemn occasions: I never cease to be thrilled when the trumpets sound from high above the nave in Westminster Abbey for the introduction to Vaughan Williams's arrangement of 'The Old Hundredth'. And when the organ crashes into the hymn 'All people that on earth do dwell/Sing to the Lord with cheerful voice' – only to be repeated with yet greater intensity by the trumpets until people, choir, organ and brass combine in the last verse in the majesty of the doxology:

> To Father, Son, and Holy Ghost,
> The God whom heaven and earth adore,
> From men and from the angel-host
> Be praise and glory evermore.

– that is one of the most glorious congregational acts of praise in Anglican music. Charles Villiers Stanford's *Te Deum* in B Flat, which I sang as a chorister in massed choirs in Canterbury Cathedral, holds a similar pre-eminence in my mind among church or cathedral music. For acts of praise I still long for hymns to be sung in Latin, as they were in Balliol Chapel when I was an undergraduate; '*Aeterna Christi munera*', to the tune of the same name, has a resonance and authority sung in Latin which is so often lacking in English hymnody. The Scottish metrical psalms have a rhythm of their own, which makes up for some of the disadvantages of congregational singing, and they are set to many of the finest tunes we possess. The old 124th has always been a favourite of mine.

Now Israel may say and that truly,

If that the Lord had not our cause maintained,

If that the Lord had not our cause sustained

When cruel men against us furiously

Rose up in wrath to make of us their prey.

Yet it is the Welsh who are commonly supposed to have some of the best tunes, and their special choral tradition is renowned. One has only to visit an Eisteddfod to discover how high the quality of their singing can be. That this kind of music-making permeates their daily lives and is a natural response to almost every occasion, there can be no doubt. I recall one instance in the summer of 1951 when the Labour Government, with a majority of only seven, had been hard-pressed throughout the session and in particular on the Finance Bill, which had been dragged out day after day and night after night, until we were finally on a Sitting that had lasted continuously for thirty-two hours. At ten o'clock one night came the last vote on the Bill. Everyone was exhausted. As Junior Whip, I went to stand by the door where the Labour Members of Parliament were being counted by my opposite number. Suddenly, as I stood there, I heard a low sound beginning to well up from the Government lobby. The doors were opened and as the Labour Members filed through, the sound grew and grew. In that moment of supreme stress and strain, the Welsh Members were singing:

Guide me, O thou great Redeemer

Pilgrim through this barren land

to the tune of *'Cwm Rhondda',* with all the passion of men and women who had reached a crucial time in their fortunes and had turned again to the childhood tunes of the Welsh valleys. As the words 'Bread of Heaven, Bread of Heaven/Feed me till I want no more' swelled out and they burst into that wonderful harmonization of 'want no more', I felt sure it was giving them the strength to carry on the battle. It is the same fervour that invariably sweeps me away when I hear a vast congregation in St Paul's Cathedral singing with thundering organ accompaniment the 'Battle Hymn of the Republic' – 'Mine eyes have seen the glory of the coming of the Lord'.

The Americans, in their 200 years of history, seem to have accumulated some of the most inspiring popular tunes, as well as some of the best student songs. The latter I have heard at Yale, sung by a group of students in the traditional way, sitting round the table with their beer mugs and without words or music, rather in the manner of German students in a beer cellar. British students are weak on this sort of singing; in my day, most could barely manage 'Drink to me only with thine eyes', or 'On Ilkley Moor 'baht 'at'. Today, I doubt that they even know those. Nor do politicians in Britain have much to do with party songs, although I have heard tell of a Socialist Song Book. 'The Red Flag' has never been accepted by the great majority of the Labour Party as other than a perfunctory nod towards left-wing aspirations; most are hard put to recall the words. The Conservatives are loath to appear to take over any of our patriotic songs for political purposes. So seldom have I heard political songs outside Communist countries that I was taken aback when crossing the Baltic on my way to a European Conference at Helsinki in 1964 to find myself listening to the Danish Foreign Minister, swaying as he stood on a chair in the dining room of a rolling ship at 2 a.m., singing to the tune of 'John Brown's body':

We'll make Nancy Astor

Sweep the stairs of Transport House.

After innumerable verses I asked his wife where he had learned this party political doggerel. 'Oh,' she replied, 'in the early days of the Movement.' Such days seem to be past. Or is it that today's political characters no longer lend themselves to this kind of musical cartoon treatment?

Film music is almost always taken for granted. When it is well done it makes its contribution to the unity of the production, but even in this subordinate role it exists as music *per se* and is absorbed into our musical consciousness. Sometimes, too, it achieves a more independent status. Arthur Bliss's music for the film of H. G. Wells's *The Shape of Things to Come* in 1935 was the first serious film score to be recognized outside the cinema. I, for one, was far more impressed by it than by the film itself, which in many ways I found unconvincing. Following that, the 'Warsaw' Concerto, used as the theme music for *Dangerous Moonlight,* and, among others in more recent times, Malcolm Arnold's haunting theme from *The Bridge on the River Kwai* or Belafonte's mesmerizing song 'Island in the Sun' have all passed into common musical language. William Walton's music for *The First of the Few,* in particular the 'Spitfire' prelude and fugue, has made a more lasting impact on me than any other film music in recent years. He himself believed that some of the best music in this genre that he had written was that for the film *The Battle of Britain,* which was discarded by the producers and has only recently been published and recorded as a suite. When I was Prime Minister I was able to persuade the film company concerned to agree to return the manuscript to Walton, and I made him a present of this agreement at his seventieth birthday party at 10 Downing Street.

So far I have dealt with music only as it appears more or less inciden-tally in our everyday life and on special occasions. But what has music meant to me in my home, in the concert hall or opera house? In my home it is, first and foremost, something that I make for myself, either by playing my Steinway or clavichord, or by using my record collection. Music enables me to express my moods and at the same time provides me with new experiences, which refresh me spiritually and help me to continue with the daily task.

In the first edition of this book I largely avoided answering the most oft-asked questions in musical conversations – those about favourite works, favourite composers, and so forth. After all, we all want to hear different works – with their different messages and the different atmos-pheres that they evoke – according to our mood and state of mind. Music may dispel a mood or enhance it; it can soothe a rage or turn con-tentment into irritation!

For instance, there are times when I want to express the sheer joy of being alive. What better way than by playing one of the early sonatas of Beethoven, Opus 10 No. 1 in C Minor, for example? Or Mozart's Sonata in A Major, No. 11 K.331, with its famous *Alla Turca* rondo for the last movement, which I played at school in a contest and which earned me the leading musical prize. Or perhaps some of Chopin's preludes or waltzes or polonaises – or even one or two of the much underestimated Mendelssohn's 'Songs without Words'. Brahms's Rhapsody in E Flat, Opus 119, allows me to turn happiness into music, while Schumann in his 'Carnival in Vienna' gives free expression to all the life and gaiety of the occasion, even slipping in bars of the *'Marseillaise'*, which at that time was forbidden music.

In more reflective mood, and feeling the need for peaceful reconciliation with myself after a day of conflict, I turn to Bach, the preludes and fugues, or perhaps Harriet Cohen's piano arrangement of '*Liebster Jesu, wir sind hier*', and Walter Rummel's of '*Ertödt uns durch dein Güte*', or the slow movements of Beethoven's sonatas. Schubert's 'Posthumous' Sonata in B Flat, or the last movement of Beethoven's last sonata, No. 111 in C Minor, all bring me particular solace, as does Brahms's simple Intermezzo in E Flat Major, Opus 117.

Nor should Schumann's miniatures like the '*Kinderszenen*' be underestimated. '*Träumerei*' – 'Dreaming' – has a marvellous simplicity, which it is unfortunately more difficult to do justice than to many a technically fiendish piece. At a concert at Carnegie Hall – his first public appearance for twelve years – Horowitz played this as one of his encores. He had recorded it in the thirties, but his performance that night showed that the man with the greatest pianistic technique since Busoni had also such supreme control that he could play '*Träumerei*', without affectation or false emphasis and allow it to speak for itself, even better than he had been able to do twenty years before. Whatever my mood, there is something for the piano to meet it.

But these are private occasions. Much of the music we enjoy is in public, in the concert hall or in the opera house. Let us approach this with the attitude that at least there will always be something of interest in a performance, and in all probability much that we can enjoy. Just occasionally there will be a performance that will remain in the memory beyond all others and which we shall be thankful not to have missed – sometimes because of the atmosphere, at others because of the personalities; sometimes because the music excels, sometimes – the rarest moments of all – when all three coalesce in a breathtaking beauty.

The memories flood back: Sir Thomas Beecham, at one of his last concerts, conducting in a chair at the Festival Hall, with Cherniavsky playing
Saint-Saëns's first Cello Concerto in A Minor, the old man's and the
young cellist's heads so close together they seemed almost to be com-
muning over the music rather than presenting a performance; Josef Krips
happily wending his way through a sublime performance of Beethoven's
'Pastoral' Symphony, placid, unhurried and unhurrying, at one with
nature, as Beethoven meant it to be; Herbert von Karajan, with the
Vienna Philharmonic Orchestra, playing Richard Strauss's *'Also sprach
Zarathustra',* the opening C Minor/B Major dissonance developing
through the wild waltz until all is reconciled in the quiet closing chords
of C Major – so stupendous was the applause that von Karajan picked up
his baton for an encore, something I had never known him do at any
other time, and to our astonishment, and to the disgust of the Austrian
Ambassador, who immediately walked out, broke into the sounds of
Johann Strauss's 'Tales from the Vienna Woods'; many, many performances by Artur Rubinstein – the Beethoven, Chopin, Brahms,
Saint-Saëns concerti – and then the generosity of his encores, very often
the resounding Polonaise in A Flat of Chopin; the Bach Choir, on a
Sunday before Easter, singing the St Matthew Passion, half before lunch
and half afterwards – and on one occasion the soprano being taken ill
just after the beginning of her first aria, when quick as a flash David
Willcocks, the conductor, brought in all the sopranos to sing the rest of
the aria from sight; Cantelli, fated to be killed in an air crash so early in
his life, who seemed more likely than anyone to follow Toscanini, producing brilliant performances, warm and not hard; Stravinsky conducting
'The Firebird' a the end of his last concert in London, his arms dropping
lower and lower as he completed the suite – we thought he would never

manage it, but in the last few moments he suddenly recovered his strength and brought it to its triumphant conclusion; afterwards he signed three sketches of himself conducting for me, writing on them, 'Not bad at all!'

—

Although every day and every mood has its own 'Desert Island Discs', I did agree a few years back to go on the programme of that name, and was forced to break cover and choose my own favoured eight works. When I was reduced to the one work to treasure above all others, I chose the Prisoners' Chorus from *Fidelio*. This has for many years seemed to me the one indispensable work, and the one that I should most dearly love to conduct. Indeed, if any single composer can be said to straddle the Classical and Romantic eras, whilst achieving true greatness and insight into the human condition, it must be Ludwig van Beethoven, whose greatest works transcend words and description as only the finest music can.

One of the most remarkable musical events in my recent experience was 'Bürger für Beethoven' in Bonn during December 1995. Beethoven was born in Bonn, and his music is played there a great deal, not least in the Beethovenhalle, where I conducted the LSO in 1975. In 1995, however, the local authority was unable to provide its usual stipendium for the winter Beethoven series, and in place of that arose a special 48-hour festival in celebration of Beethoven's 225th anniversary, organized by the people of Bonn. The festival began on a Friday night with the BBC Symphony Orchestra and Chorus performing the Mass in D and then continued solidly, day and night, until the Sunday evening. During the small hours, artists of the highest calibre played chamber music and sang songs by Beethoven, mainly in the renovated Beethovenhaus in the city centre; by day there were further recitals, and each evening there were orchestral concerts. Between 11 p.m. on Saturday night and 1 a.m. on Sunday morning, the distinguished Polish composer Penderecki conducted superb performances of the Violin Concerto and the Seventh Symphony in a packed church in the centre of town.

The festival was to close with a mammoth orchestral concert conducted by Lorin Maazel, who once conducted all of Beethoven's symphonies in a single day on London's South Bank. I considered it an enormous honour when I was invited to open the festival with a speech about Beethoven, and I found it both moving and instructive to revisit his life and works in order to gather my thoughts for such an occasion.

The history of our continent has been a bloody one, repeatedly despoiled by war, invasion and counter-invasion, revolution and all the human misery that comes with them. But a few remarkable men stand out far above all of that, and none more than Beethoven. His works are perhaps unique in that they somehow not only represent a fresh musical school, but also epitomize a new philosophy – of social solidarity, and of the brotherhood between men. The works of Beethoven can both powerfully evoke their time and yet transcend it; and what a turbulent historical background confronted their writer – the dissolution of the Habsburg Empire, the French Revolution and the Napoleonic Wars. When first hearing the works of Beethoven, who has not wondered what kind of man could have composed such masterpieces, and what kind of period could have produced him?

There can surely be no other musician to compare, as a man, with Beethoven. Who could fail to be moved by his titanic character, his disdain of the protocols of society, his growing deafness, his dedication of the 'Eroica' and its subsequent, passionate destruction, the Heiligenstadt

Testament and all the other features of a life of such moral and creative strength? Like so many of his period, Beethoven drew inspiration from the brilliant characters of Homer, Plutarch and Shakespeare and from the democratic political revolutions of his time – yet he himself had a reputation for abrasiveness and rudeness. This was one of many contradictions in this extraordinary man, who, for all his scorn of society's mores, never dropped his 'van', with its hint of aristocratic superiority. As a young man he was already regarded as more than a little arrogant and sure of himself – and somewhat lofty. As the aged Haydn saw less and less of the busy young composer, he would ask of common acquaintances: 'How goes it with our Great Mogul?'

Perhaps it is impossible to imagine the greatness without the loftiness, the sudden and wonderful bursts of creative activity without the impatience, the genius without the flaws. Nor must we forget that Beethoven was himself frustrated and troubled by his difficulties in dealing with other people – he desperately wanted his social graces to match his philosophical ideals, but his impatience and his growing deafness so often got the better of him. His deeply personal and confessional Testament of Heiligenstadt gives us all a moving insight into the internal struggles that accompanied his immense creativity. Above all else, it reassures us of what we already know – that the composer of *Fidelio* was moved by love of his fellow men. Indeed, although he composed relatively little for it, the human voice usually brought out the best in Beethoven.

It is as well to be wary of drawing close parallels between political events and musical developments, but there can be no doubt that Beethoven was strongly influenced by liberal thought. For the bracing wind of freedom was already blowing strongly from the West – from the new Republic of America, from France and from the philosophers of

England; and Beethoven rejoiced in it. There can be no more potent, more moving expression of freedom than *Fidelio* – to my mind by far the greatest opera mankind has wrought. Politicians and philosophers may squabble about the true nature of freedom, and many will always subvert its slogans and concepts to suit their own ends. But true freedoms – freedom of thought and expression, freedom from the knock on the door in the dead of night, freedom from nuisance and harassment, freedom to develop and to live a fulfilling life – these are the freedoms that continue to inspire me in politics, and they are the ideals that inspired Beethoven and his generation.

In the introduction to his marvellous autobiography, Bruno Walter wrote: 'Napoleon is dead – but Beethoven lives'. How right he was. For so long as *Fidelio* is played and loved, for so long as the tones of Beethoven's late string quartets are heard, then the human soul is somehow free, and alive. Although a man so modest would never even have thought of adding this, it should also be said that Bruno Walter himself lives on too. He lives in the hearts of those who, like myself, had the privilege of meeting him and hearing his concerts – and with those people who are acquainted with the very characteristic humility and warmth of his recorded performances. The ideals that were embodied by these great men of the past are still alive, and still relevant.

Ludwig van Beethoven's ninth and final symphony, culminating in that huge, epoch-making setting of the 'Ode to Joy', is also much more than just a piece of music. Schiller's lines, like Beethoven's music, were of their time and yet of all time. This is truly an explosion of joy, and an expression of all that is positive in human nature, and of course it gave us one of the irresistible themes of all music, now the European anthem. When Germany was at last reunited and the scar of the post-war settlement was wiped from across its heart, it was an appropriate and poignant choice when Leonard Bernstein came from London to Berlin to conduct the Ninth Symphony of Beethoven. He conducted an orchestra drawn from across Europe, and from the United States, and in the final chorus he substituted 'Freiheit' for 'Freude'. It is believed that a rather disreputable nineteenth-century political figure by the name of Friedrich Ludwig Jahn alleged that Schiller himself once toyed with such wording. But on Christmas Day 1989 nobody was greatly concerned about the historical accuracy of this story. The power of that concert was too great, and the power of Beethoven to bring healing and reconciliation was again celebrated, with the world looking on. The spirit of Beethoven was abroad that Christmas.

As it happens, the finest and most memorable performance that I have ever heard was of one of Beethoven's greatest works, in the Albert Hall on 28 September 1963. To begin with, it was imprinted on my memory because it started at 9.15 p.m. – late for a concert in the post-war years. I went because three violinists, Yehudi Menuhin and the Oistrakhs, father and son, were playing, taking it turn and turn about to play together or to conduct. That night, with the Moscow Philharmonic Orchestra conducted by David Oistrakh, Yehudi Menuhin played Beethoven's Violin Concerto in D. I have long admired him as a man for his wide and varied interests, as well as for his playing. We have written innumerable letters to each other about the problems of the world and the future of mankind. That night at the Albert Hall it seemed at times as though his concern with these matters was inspiring his playing; he produced such purity of tone, such breadth of style and such a depth of interpretation that I was transported beyond the surroundings of the concert hall into another world; I doubt whether I shall ever hear Beethoven's Violin

Concerto played in the same way again. It was an experience not just for that evening but one that will remain with me for the rest of my life, for in Menuhin's hands the music became a profound embodiment of human values; and it is something upon which I can draw when I contemplate such higher matters.

Only on rare occasions will a combination of circumstances make such performances possible; nevertheless, they represent something towards which every musician should aspire. Many of the conditions necessary for this pursuit of excellence may, in themselves, appear to be run-of-the-mill, humdrum matters: at what age children should start to learn how to play instruments; how their general education should be combined with specialization in music; how the performer may avoid the tensions of insecurity, yet, at the same time, be spurred on to ever greater artistry. But this is true of all human affairs. We no longer accept that the impoverished garret is the *sine qua non* of artistic endeavour. The place of the artist in society is now well recognized. It rests with artists themselves to ensure that neither their creative urge nor their keenness in performance is blurred by the distractions of our material world.

The written word and the spoken word tell their own story. But, while a picture can be adequately described to those who know the world around them without their actually seeing it, there is a limit to what words can achieve in describing musical perfection. The structure, the instrumentation, the history, the purpose, the life of the composer and the executant – all these can be put into words; but at this point words exhaust their usefulness. There is nothing further they can do. The music remains. It is only the music that can then work its miracle on each of us, if we give it the chance. For all who give it their feeling and understanding, music will remain a joy for ever.

COLLECTING –
A PERSONAL GUIDE
———

The purpose of this book is an intensely personal one – to share with its readers some of the sheer joy that music has brought to me. This chapter is not an attempt to list exhaustively the great composers, their major works, and the finest recordings made of them. However, I felt it would be useful to include a personal guide to performances of the works I love most, in the hope that the reader will also find the intense and lifelong joy that music has to offer.

Thanks to the growing affordability and availability of compact discs, classical music is one of the most accessible forms of art today – and the enthusiast can choose between a whole range of equally valid, but quite different, interpretations of the classical repertoire. My aim is to suggest a list of recordings that have given me particular pleasure (references are correct at the time of going to press, but may be subject to change). This highly subjective process will undoubtedly incite debate, but these arguments should be largely beneficial as we seek to gain an insight into the different conceptions of these works.

Few can deny the importance of a Beethoven symphony, but a specific conductor's interpretation of one of these works will be open to criticism and praise from all sides. In this fact lies much of the joy of music collecting. After one has had the experience of listening to Furtwängler or Bernstein conducting Beethoven's Fifth Symphony and then hearing Toscanini, George Szell or Günter Wand do this piece, it would virtually be impossible to think of it as the same work. But all these views are valid in their own way. The differences that arise embody the essence of music collecting. There is no simple answer, and without the composer to consult we are at liberty to come to our own conclusions – none of which are necessarily right or wrong.

I hope that the amateur can use this chapter as a guide to the major composers in Western music and their works. I hope too that professionals will find it productive, in provoking them to explore specific performances from which I have derived countless hours of enjoyment.

The past twenty years have witnessed a real explosion of 'period' or 'authentic' performances. This is not something that has great appeal for me. I take the view that if you want to pass through what you conceive as historic emotions, then you are entitled to do so. I am not interested in doing so myself, because I do not think it produces the best results. When people say that they want to do Beethoven, for example, in its original form, I ask myself this very simple question: 'If Beethoven were alive today, would he want to play on that little Broadwood piano he had in Bonn, or would he prefer to play on the latest Steinway?' I have no doubt what his choice would be, and that is my choice as well. I cannot help feeling that people who want to do this historical look-back are really trying to escape the responsibilities of modern instruments, modern orchestras or modern technology. They want to escape from it all so they dash back, find some cubbyhole where there is an instrument and say: 'Look how clever we are, we are really in the seventeenth century.' This allows certain groups of musicians and conductors to put their individual stamp on items they are recording, and because others are tired of the modern world, they get support. But it is not my sort of thing.

The quintessential Italian baroque musician, ANTONIO VIVALDI

(1678–1741) was a well-known violinist and composer in his own time, who wrote more than 400 concerti. He was also responsible for dozens of operas and several religious works. The piece of his that is most often performed is a set of four violin concerti entitled *The Four Seasons*. There are many performances available on CD, but one very good recommendation is the best-selling recording by Nigel Kennedy and the English Chamber Orchestra on EMI Classics (CDC 749 557 2).

Largely a self-taught musician, JOHANN SEBASTIAN BACH (1685–1750) was little known in his time outside a specialist circle. Now he is widely recognized as the father of Western music. He pushed the limits of baroque convention to their extreme and was responsible for influencing countless other great masters who followed in later years. His inventive creations and daring style are regarded as the foundation of modern harmony. Many of his works derived from his religious inspi-ration, which was an integral part of his prolific life, and a recent recording by one of the finest English conductors shows how effectively the energy, and the spiritual qualities, of one of Bach's greatest pieces, the B Minor Mass, can be captured on a recording without resort to the extremes of 'period performance' that I deplore (Hickox, CHAN 0533/4).

Singing in a choir means automatically that you take part in the works of Bach, Handel, Haydn and the nineteenth-century composers. Learning the organ when my voice broke, I was very much occupied with Bach and others who wrote for the organ. When I was at Oxford as an undergraduate singing in the Bach Choir, we did all the early composers as well as the modern ones. There are many works that I learned then and in which I rejoice, such as Bach's St Matthew Passion and the St John Passion, which I have often sung but never conducted. Both works have been recorded often, but it is certainly possible to single out a fine recording by Georg Solti of the St Matthew Passion (Decca 421 177-2) and a truly classic one of the St John Passion conducted by Benjamin Britten (Decca 443 859-2). Both works are also available in delightful recordings conducted by Peter Schreier, which have a pleasing lightness of touch, again without that period performance dogma (both on Philips – 412 527-2 and 422 088-2, respectively). Perhaps even more ethereally beautiful, there is also Bach's motet *'Jesu meine Freude'*, which I sang with the Bach Choir in the chapel at St George's, Windsor in 1938. There are fine motet collections available from both EMI and Philips.

Alongside those larger choral works, he contributed much in the form of cantatas for solo voice, and all of these have been recorded by conductors such as Nikolaus Harnoncourt and Karl Richter. Bach's final creation, *The Art of Fugue,* is a collection of fugues all based on the same theme and is regarded as one of the greatest masterpieces ever written for the keyboard. Of his concerti, the Harpsichord Concerti, as recorded by Igor Kipnis with Neville Marriner and the London Strings (Sony SB2K53243), are among the best. The Brandenburg Concerti are well-known works for small chamber groups featuring various instruments, and are available in a wide range of recordings and playing styles. But surely no recording can be more affectionate or moving than Yehudi Menuhin's with the Bath Festival Orchestra, available at a bargain price from EMI (CES 568 516 2). Bach also made a huge contribution in the form of solo keyboard (usually organ) works, which consist mostly of chorales, culminating in the forty-eight preludes and fugues for the clavier – the predecessor of the harpsichord and then the piano – known as *The Well-Tempered Clavier* (Sviatoslav Richter, RCA GD60949).

Born in Germany, GEORG FRIEDRICH HANDEL (1685–1759) eventually became a British citizen and took up residence in London, where he

189

flourished as an organist and composer. He lived quite an eccentric lifestyle and was a very popular figure in his own time. Today, the Germans and the British still argue about which country can more credibly claim Handel as one of its own, as I discovered when I was in Germany at the Schleswig-Holstein Music Festival and finished conducting Beethoven's Eighth Symphony. They kept on applauding, so I said that we would play some of the *Water Music* by that well-known British composer, Georg Friedrich Handel. A gasp went up from the audience. Having finished the concert, we were all having drinks outside when a young man came up to me and asked me very politely if I would sign his programme. I obliged. When I handed it back to him, he changed completely and snarled at me: 'And *Händel* is not a British composer!'

Handel produced a huge variety of music, writing for almost every available genre. Despite – or perhaps because of – the range of his work, only a small portion is heard today. One of his most enjoyable works is the *Water Music* (Malcolm, ECO, ASV Dig. CDQS 6152), which I have conducted on a number of occasions. I have also conducted the *Messiah* (available in a fine performance including Kiri Te Kanawa, Georg Solti and the Chicago Symphony Orchestra, on Decca 414 396-2), some of the organ concerti and the 'Arrival of the Queen of Sheba' (from the oratorio *Solomon),* the last of which is now available on my own CD from EMI (5 66063 2). Amongst his oratorios, *Israel in Egypt* and *Theodora* contain some of his finest work. Although not his most serious endeavour, the *Music for Royal Fireworks* (Marriner, ASMF, Decca 4145962) is reminiscent of the great tradition of early British music. The *Concerti Grossi,* for small orchestra, warmly recorded by my Balliol scholar contemporary and good friend George Malcolm (ASV CDDC-S303) are regarded by many as the high point of baroque orchestral music.

JOSEPH HAYDN (1732–1809) is perhaps the archetypal classical composer. He was born at the end of the baroque era, and lived to see the birth of Romanticism. He is largely responsible for developing and stabilizing the popularity of the modern symphony. Symphonies certainly represent a large portion of his musical output, as he wrote 104 of them! I find his late symphonies as enjoyable as any other orchestral works of this era, and they are available from Decca in a series of vigorous recordings made by the London Philharmonic conducted by Georg Solti (Decca 436 290-2). Of his string quartets, my favourites are the Opus 54 group, particularly the one in G Major, especially well performed by the Amadeus Quartet (DG 437 134-2). Written very late in his life, *The Seasons,* which I sang in the Bach Choir at Oxford in 1936, (Marriner, PHIL 438 715-2PM2) contains many excellent examples of Haydn's musical genius, while his magnificent *Creation* (Solti, CSO, Philips 443 445-2) for orchestra, soloists and chorus presents some of the most beautiful music written for voice in the classical era. I once conducted this work in the Town Hall at Oxford, a most enjoyable occasion.

A Haydn concerto is often a vital part of any instrumentalist's repertoire. The Concerto for Keyboard and Orchestra in D (Argerich, EMI CDM7 63575-2) and the Trumpet Concerto in E Flat (Hånan Hardenberger Philips 420 203-2) are two of the most popular. His cello concerti, and particularly the Cello Concerto in C, are beautifully played by my friend, Mstislav Rostropovich, with the Academy of St Martin-in-the-Fields on a reissued CD (EMI CDC 749 305-2).

WOLFGANG AMADEUS MOZART (1756–91) began his career as one of the most remarkable of the world's child prodigies, and died at the early age of thirty-five, leaving behind a huge amount of some of the most beautiful music ever written. His life was wrought with heartbreak, sickness, financial insecurity and finally the prophetic fear that the requiem mass he was writing in his last days would be his own. Amidst the many troubles of his short life, he managed to write some of history's finest piano concerti. Murray Perahia has recorded all of these and his performances are of a uniformly high quality (Sony S12K46441). But a good starting point with these concerti is probably a bargain-priced double CD of the late concerti as recorded by Alfred Brendel (Marriner, ASMF, Philips Duo 442 269-2). Mozart's concerti for other instruments are also very fine works. Isaac Stern has recorded all the violin concerti (Sony SM3K66475), a set still unsurpassed after thirty years. Dennis Brain, the virtuoso horn player, produced the definitive recordings of the horn concerti (von Karajan, EMI CDC 555 087-2), and the Concerto for Clarinet and Orchestra in A is still available on a classic recording by Jack Brymer with Sir Thomas Beecham conducting (EMI CDM 763408-2).

Mozart's contribution to the world of orchestral music must not be underrated. Although his sheer output did not equal that of his close friend Joseph Haydn, I believe that his last two symphonies (Nos 40 and 41, Szell, Sony SBK46333) rank among the best examples of what was achieved at the height of the classical era.

No collection of music could be complete without the presence of some Mozart operas. Nowadays *Die Zauberflöte* is perhaps his best-known opera, and its memorable themes and glorious arias certainly make it one of my favourite Mozart creations. I am not convinced that the recording made in Berlin by Sir Thomas Beecham in 1937 will ever be equalled (Pearl GEMMCDS 9371). His other operas include *Don Giovanni* (Giulini, EMI CDS7 47260-8), *Die Entführung aus dem Serail* (Solti, 417 402-2), *Così fan tutte* (Solti, Decca 444 174-2) and *Le Nozze di Figaro* (Böhm, DG 449-728-2). Bruno Walter has recorded a number of Mozart overtures, which I also enjoy listening to when there is not time for an entire opera.

Mozart wrote many settings of the Mass, and I have always enjoyed the *Mass in C Minor* (Bernstein, DG 431 791-2). Finally, his last work, the *Mass in D Minor 'Requiem'* (in a fine recording by Peter Schreier on Philips 411 420-2) was indeed unfinished due to the composer's death, and exists in a number of completions.

LUDWIG VAN BEETHOVEN (1770–1827) is arguably the most important single person in musical history. When he began his life as a composer, the Classical era was ending and his music was not far removed from that of Haydn. By the end of his life, the world had witnessed the beginning of the Romantic era, emanating largely from the pen of this great man. Although he started to lose his hearing in his mid-twenties, he proceeded to turn out masterpiece after masterpiece. For the last ten years of his life he had lost all hearing but continued to compose.

Beethoven's music has always played a large role in my life. I have regularly conducted several of his symphonies. My favourite is probably the Eighth Symphony, which I have conducted on many occasions, including a concert with the Chicago Symphony Orchestra and, most notably, one with the English Chamber Orchestra in the chapel of the Royal Naval College at Greenwich, as part of the Japanese Praemium Imperiale Festival in 1995. I also chose to feature it in our programme when I was on tour with the London Concert Orchestra in 1984. I think it is a fine symphony – and some scholars say that it is the best of all the Beethoven symphonies – but at the same time one of the least appreciated. Some people believe it is a small and simple symphony. In fact, it is quite complicated and difficult to play accurately. It is seldom performed in concert halls in Britain, and whenever I have conducted it we have been rewarded with a very positive response.

Many recordings of Beethoven's symphonies have been made over the years. Of the complete sets, I have found the best to be that made by Herbert von Karajan with the Berlin Philharmonic Orchestra in the early sixties (DG 429 036-2). More recently, Günter Wand has also produced an excellent digital set, which is an outstanding bargain (RCA 74321 20277-2). Furthermore, his live recordings of the Fifth and Sixth symphonies (BMG/RCA Dig. 09026 61930-2) are among the most energetic and moving performances on record. The Seventh Symphony has been memorably recorded by Arturo Toscanini (RCA GD60253) in mono sound, but I do not believe anyone has been able to improve upon the performance. Finally, Beethoven's most triumphant work, the Ninth Symphony, has been masterfully interpreted several times by von Karajan, probably most effectively in the mid-seventies (DG 415 832-2).

I have already written about Beethoven's only opera, *Fidelio,* and I could not easily live with only one recorded performance of it, although the greatest is probably an EMI set recorded over thirty years ago by Otto Klemperer (EMI CDS 555 170-2). I have seen many performances of this work and have encountered varying degrees of success. Most recently I watched a performance at the Summer Festival in Salzburg, where they completely ignored Beethoven's intentions. It was well sung and played, but the setting was quite inadequate and the staging revealed a complete lack of understanding on the part of the producers as to what it was all about and what Beethoven had intended. I look back with joy to the first production of *Fidelio* that was put on at Glyndebourne in 1959, with Gui conducting. And this music of freedom has never ceased to move me.

The great Ukrainian pianist Sviatoslav Richter has a wonderful

—

ability to interpret Beethoven's piano works, and I always enjoy his strong performances (several sonatas – PHIL 438 486-2; Eroica Variations – OLYM OCD339). All five piano concerti have been skilfully played with just the right combination of flair and poetry by Krystian Zimerman and the Vienna Philharmonic (DG Dig. 435 467-2), and I doubt whether the Violin Concerto has ever been more beautifully played than by Yehudi Menuhin (Furtwängler, EMI CDH7 69799-2).

I have always been a supporter of Beethoven's Triple Concerto for Violin, Cello and Piano, but despite its many fine passages, it is only seldom performed. The slow movement always brings tears to my eyes, and it can be as moving as anything that this great man wrote when it is played by a genuine trio who work together on a regular basis. I recorded this concerto in 1988 with the Trio Zingara – Felix Schmidt, Annette Cole and Elizabeth Layton – and the English Chamber Orchestra, and I am very proud that this is still seen as one of the finest performances available (IMP/Carlton 30367 0091-2). Indeed, soon after the CD was released, I received a very complimentary letter from von Karajan congratulating me on a superb performance of a work that he himself had twice recorded.

Some of my other favourite works are the 'Archduke' Trio, Opus 97 (Cortot, Thiband, Casals EMI CDH 761 024-2), and the *Missa Solemnis* (Bernstein, Sony SM2K47522).

Despite his short life and virtual lack of public recognition, FRANZ SCHUBERT (1797–1828) is now regarded as a supreme master. He was incredibly hard working and produced an amazing amount of music in such a short life. So long as he was composing music, he stayed relatively happy and avoided the mental turmoil to which countless other composers fell prey.

I have always loved his symphonies, particularly his Fifth Symphony (No. 3, No. 5, and No. 6 – Beecham, Royal PO, EMI CDM7 69750-2) and the Eighth Symphony *'Unfinished'* (No. 8 and No. 9 – Wand, Berlin PO, RCA 09026 68314-2), and have often conducted them. His Ninth is the greatest symphony of its period, and I have the happiest memories of conducting it once at the Windsor Festival.

Schubert also wrote some of the most delightful chamber music including the B Flat Trio (Cortot, Thibaud, Casals, EMI CDH 761 024-2) and the Piano Quintet in A Major 'The Trout' (Brendel, Philips 400 078-2). He also wrote hundreds of songs for voice and piano, my favourite of which is the song cycle, *Die Winterreise* (Pears and Britten, Decca 417 473-2).

HECTOR BERLIOZ (1803–69) was one of the first in a long line of great Romantic French composers. To sum up the life of Berlioz one need only examine his relationship with Harriet Smithson, a young Irish actress. After seeing her in a play, Berlioz became what today might be known as a stalker. Even though they did not share a common language, he sent her a barrage of love letters, followed her around, and tried to impress her with his music, all of which led her to terror instead of love. After a failed relationship with another woman, Berlioz again took up his infatuation with Harriet, a process of courtship that climaxed with a failed suicide attempt and then miraculously ended in their marriage.

As one of the strongest supporters of programme music, he modelled most of his works on poems, books and art. I have always been wary of this type of music, because sometimes the music depends so heavily upon its inspiration that it loses its power and effect without that accompanying piece of art. Despite this, there is still much to enjoy in the music of Berlioz, particularly his *Symphonie Fantastique* (Bernstein, FNO,

EMI CDM7 64630-2). His dramatic symphony, *Roméo et Juliette* (Toscanini, RCA GD60274) contains some incredibly beautiful music, and is greatly undervalued today.

FELIX MENDELSSOHN (1809–47) grew up in Germany and, in the eyes of many, was seemingly destined to be another Mozart. He was almost as impressive a child prodigy and his aspirations were high. He eventually settled himself with a wife and a prestigious appointment, with which he helped found a conservatory in Leipzig where he could teach and compose.

His gift for melody sets him apart from many other composers of his era. His Symphony No. 4 'Italian' (Szell, Cleveland, Sony SBK46536) is the finest of his orchestral works and represents the full range of his talents, and still has great public appeal. His concerti are also notable, as are the virtuosic performances of them by some of the finest talents of this century (Violin Concerto – Heifetz, Beecham, EMI CDH5 65191-2; Moura Lympany's performance of Piano Concerto No. 1, currently deleted). His Songs Without Words (Barenboim, DG 523 931-2) are particularly beautiful, as is his oratorio, *Elijah* (Frühbeck de Burgos, EMI CZS5 68601-2).

Although FREDERIC CHOPIN (1810–49) was limited in the scope of his compositions (he wrote almost entirely for solo piano), he was a hugely influential figure in early Romantic music, highly regarded in his time as a pianist as well as a composer. His works created the need for several advances in piano technique, which have since become standard for any pianist. Although they are amongst his best-known works, his piano concerti are not particularly well orchestrated – they are primarily works for the piano. His First Piano Concerto (actually the second he wrote) was one of the few works recorded by the great Dinu Lipatti before his tragic death (EMI CDH 763 497-2), and his CD of solo piano works is also a deeply moving testament to a man of quite extraordinary technical gifts as well as sensibility (EMI CDH 769 802-2). My own preference, however, is for Chopin's Piano Concerto No. 2 (poetically played by Ivo Pogorelich on DG 410 507-2), which I have had the pleasure of performing with Ivo on two occasions.

After a debilitating disease left him without the full use of all his fingers, ROBERT SCHUMANN (1810–56) abandoned his dreams of being a piano performer and became more serious about composing. His career was soon invigorated by his much-debated marriage to Clara Wieck, which left Schumann happy and able to produce exquisite music. Like most composers, though, his happiness was short-lived. His mental problems quickly worsened and he sought peace at the bottom of the Rhine, but was rescued and placed in an institution where he wasted away. In the short time when he was a productive composer, Schumann wrote an excellent piano concerto (Fleisher, Sony MPK44849), some marvellous songs (Dichterliebe, Pears and Britten, 443 933-2) and some memorable symphonies (available in several very splendid full sets, all on two CDs – notably those of von Karajan, on DG 429 672-2, and Wolfgang Sawallisch, on EMI CMS 764 815-2). My favourite recording of Symphony No. 4 is the famous one with Furtwängler and the Berlin Philharmonic, but this is temporarily unavailable and a good alternative is Günter Wand's NDR recording on BMG (RD60826).

FRANZ LISZT (1811–86) was probably the greatest natural pianist ever known. He also influenced piano literature and technique more than any other composer in history. He lived a long life and composed prolifically. He was also a deep thinker in the areas of philosophy and religion. He was one of the prime movers in the movement towards new music and against composers like Brahms, who embraced styles of the past. His most memorable works are those for piano, and his most popular are probably his concertante works for piano and orchestra: his splendid *Totentanz* and his two piano concerti are available on a first-class single CD (Ozawa, Zimerman, DG Dig. 423 571-2). Amongst the huge amount of solo piano literature that he produced, my favourite is the B Minor Sonata, marvellously played by my friend, Ivo Pogorelich (DG 429 391-2).

CÉSAR FRANCK (1822–90) can be seen as being over-romantic, so much so that he isolated himself from such contemporaries as Saint-Saëns and Gounod. Almost all his music was very unpopular while he was alive, but few could deny his importance and influence as a teacher and his brilliance as a keyboard performer. I have conducted his Symphonic Variations for Piano and Orchestra several times with my friend, Moura Lympany, and I believe that she has produced the finest recording of this piece, sadly deleted now. His other most notable work is the Symphony in D, which has been wonderfully recorded and paired on a CD with the Lalo Symphony in G Minor (Beecham, EMI CDM763396-2).

CAMILLE SAINT-SAËNS (1835–1921) was extremely popular in his day, thanks to his extraordinary gifts as a pianist, organist and composer. He was already an accomplished and well-known pianist by his early teens, and by his twenties his compositions had earned him great respect and admiration throughout France. He lived a long life, during which he wrote a great deal, although his compositions almost dried up during his final years. Despite this, he continued to speak out against the trends of new music whenever possible. His most popular work is his Symphony No. 3 'Organ Symphony' (Tortelier, CHAN 8822). I have always liked his Piano Concerto No. 4, although it is not his most popular, and all five of them are skilfully performed by Pascal Róge on a double CD set (Decca 443 865-2). It happens often in history that an artist becomes inexorably linked with a work with which he never intended to be forever associated. Some of the most famous examples are Handel's *Music for the Royal Fireworks,* Elgar's *Pomp and Circumstance March,* Ravel's *Bolero,* Walton's 'Spitfire' Prelude and Fugue, Khachaturian's *Sabre Dance,* Bizet's 'Toreador Song' from *Carmen* (which he wrote just to show that if the public really wanted bad music, then he could really write it!), and perhaps most famously, Saint-Saëns and the *Carnival of the Animals.* He never wanted this curiosity to be released, yet now we cannot help but associate him with this work.

RICHARD WAGNER (1813–83) had a truly profound influence on the face of Western music. He saw himself as a god and treated everyone else as his disciple or his enemy. He was undeniably a genius, but was obsessed with the drive to produce a complete work of art that would supersede all those before it and overshadow all those that could ever follow. He found that through opera he could best relay his ideas in music and poetry. His most famous work is the sixteen-hour, four-opera cycle entitled *Der Ring des Nibelungen* (Solti, Decca 414 100-2). *The Ring* is still one of the works of art most often written about today. I also particularly enjoy Wagner's opera *Die Meistersinger von Nürnberg* (von Karajan, EMI CDS 749 683-2), and have often conducted its overture. Another of his great operatic works is his version of the legend of *Tristan und Isolde* (Furtwängler, EMI CDS747322-8).

ANTON BRUCKNER (1824–96) began his musical career as a church organist and only later in life became a true symphonist. Many of his works draw on two sources of inspiration: his dedication to God and Wagner. Bruckner regarded his *Te Deum* (von Karajan, DG 429 980-2) as his finest work, and I have to agree with him on this point. As for his symphonies, if they are given time and careful consideration, I have found them to be hugely rewarding. My personal favourite is probably the Fourth Symphony, and in particular a performance by the Berlin Philharmonic conducted by Furtwängler, which has been intermittently available on lesser-known CD labels and deserves a proper re-release. Perhaps the most impressive modern recording, from the shimmering strings of the opening to the transcendental tutti of the finale, is that by Günter Wand and his North German Radio Orchestra (RCA RD60784).

There is, however, an excellent transfer available from EMI of Furtwängler conducting the Vienna Philharmonic in the Fifth Symphony (CDH 565 750 2). For many people, Symphony No. 7 is the most accessible and enjoyable of Bruckner's canon, and I still have a special affection for Herbert von Karajan's first recording with the Berlin Philharmonic Orchestra (EMI CDM7 69923-2). Choosing a recording of Symphony No. 8 is a complex matter, for there are several performing editions of the work as well as several fundamentally different ways of interpreting this supreme example of Bruckner's technique. Herbert von Karajan made a wonderfully rugged recording with the Berlin Philharmonic in the fifties, which is now available at bargain price (EMI CES 569 092 2). He recorded the work again twice, and his final recording, with the Vienna Philharmonic, is a remarkably moving document (DG Dig. 427 611-2). There are other fine recordings from Giulini (DG Dig. 445 529-2) and from Günter Wand, recorded live in a resonant but deeply affecting performance in Lübeck Cathedral (RD60364). A favourite recording of Bruckner's unfinished Symphony No. 9 is that by Bernstein and the Vienna Philharmonic Orchestra (DG Dig. 435 350-2).

Bruckner was also responsible for some of the finest settings of the

Mass written since Mozart, which are available in a specially priced and deeply moving set from Deutsche Grammophon (Jochum, Bavarian Radio SO and Choir, DG 447 409-2).

JOHANNES BRAHMS (1833–97) was writing music as the age of Romanticism was coming to an end. Many composers in this era, such as Wagner and Liszt, saw Brahms as old fashioned and developed their own style in direct contrast to all he was associated with. Despite this large group of adverse and influential critics, Brahms was quite well appreciated in his time, and today his works are seen as the culmination of the Romantic era. His popularity was partly due to the support and encouragement of Robert and Clara Schumann, with whom Brahms lived for some time.

I have conducted the works of Brahms a number of times, particularly the Academic Festival Overture (available in a live recording with the European Community Youth Orchestra, of which I am particularly proud – EMI 5 66063 2) and the *Haydn Variations*. I would have liked to do his piano concerti (No. 1 – Clifford Curzon, LSO, Szell, Decca 425 082-2; No. 2 – Koracevich, EMI CDC 555 218 2), but they are some of the most demanding works in the piano repertoire and none of the pianists I have conducted has wanted to perform them. I have, however, conducted his Double Concerto for Violin and Cello, with Yehudi Menuhin and Felix Schmidt as soloists. His symphonies (Wand at bargain price on RCA 74321 20283-2) and Violin Concerto (Ormandy, Stern, Sony SBK46335) have always been some of my favourites, and are available at a competitive price in excellent performances. They are deceptively difficult works to perform well. Perhaps the finest of Brahms's compositions is his *German Requiem* (Klemperer, EMI CDC 747 238-2). Unlike the traditional requiem based on the Latin Mass,

Brahms's requiem is based on a text by Martin Luther and is a solace for those who live on after loved ones have passed. This was the first requiem written in German, hence its name *Ein Deutsches Requiem,* and I believe it best portrays the genius of Brahms.

PETER ILYICH TCHAIKOVSKY (1840–93) is widely regarded as the greatest Russian composer ever. Although his music reflects Western European influences more often than some of his countrymen thought was acceptable, his music is undeniably and unashamedly Russian. Tchaikovsky lived a torrid and tormented life, beset by numerous mental ailments and obsessed with the morbid. Despite this, he produced some of the most beautiful music written in the nineteenth century. His Fourth, Fifth and Sixth symphonies have been widely recorded – but never more movingly than by the then Leningrad Philharmonic in the mid-fifties (Sanderling No. 4, Mravinsky Nos 5 and 6, DG 447 423-2). Tchaikovsky also wrote two of the most popular concerti in existence today. His First Piano Concerto is magnificently performed by Horowitz and Toscanini (BMG/RCA GD 60321); and the Violin Concerto has been inspirationally recorded by one of the new generation of Russian violin virtuosi, Maxim Vengerov (Teldec 4509 90881-2).

Still the most important Czech composer to date, ANTONIN DVOŘÁK (1841–1904) was strongly associated with the 'bohemian' movement and utilized folk tunes from his native land and from places he visited. Dvořák went to America for some time and was particularly influenced by the Black and Native North American musical cultures. I have played Dvořák's Ninth Symphony all over the world. There is obviously a great affinity towards this piece in Britain and the United States, but it is also very well received in the Far East. It is one of the few pieces that seems to transcend all cultural and geographical barriers and appeals to people worldwide. I particularly enjoy the recordings of the New World Symphony and the Cello Concerto from the thirties, which have been brilliantly transferred to CD by Michael Dutton (Czech PO, DUTT CDEA5002), played by Pablo Casals and conducted by Szell. Slava Rostropovich has also recorded an excellent version of the Cello Concerto with von Karajan (DG 447 413-2).

GIUSEPPE VERDI (1813–1901) wrote some of the world's best-loved operas, both in his time and in ours. After several mediocre attempts to produce a successful opera, he finally began his climb to fame. It is rare for a man to live such a normal life and yet produce so many great works. His finest include *Aida* (von Karajan, EMI CMS7 69300-2), *Il Trovatore* (Giulini, DG Dig. 423 858-2) and *La Traviata* (Solti, Decca 448 119-2). His only popular work not written for the opera house is the *Requiem* (Giulini, EMI CDS7 47257-8), which is truly a splendid work, and so dramatic that it is often described as his greatest opera! Other notable Verdi operas include *Otello,* whose title-role Placido Domingo has so famously made his own (Levine, BMG/RCA CD 82951) and *Falstaff* (Solti, Decca 417 168 2), Verdi's last opera and a remarkable product of his old age.

EDVARD GRIEG (1843–1907) is perhaps the best-known Norwegian composer to date. His music strongly reflected the rich history of his nation and sang its praises. He was adored by his country and was truly a national hero in his own time. His Piano Concerto (Fleisher, Sony MPK44849) is his most familiar work and is standard fare for any pianist today. His role in Norwegian music was very similar to the role of Sir Edward Elgar in British music early in the twentieth century. They both not only revitalized their country's music, but also created a nationalistic unity that spread far beyond the realm of classical music.

A similarly nationalistic composer was the great Finn JEAN SIBELIUS (1865–1957), who is often considered to be the greatest symphonist of the twentieth century. He specialized in orchestral music and wrote seven symphonies (Sir Colin Davis, Boston SO, Philips 446 157-2 and Philips 446 160-2), several tone poems and a violin concerto (Heifetz, EMI CDH 764 030 2). His music evokes his homeland's national spirit and he often draws on Nordic folklore and legend as the basis for it. His country's political turmoil in the twenties overflowed into his own personal life and resulted in the death of his brother. Soon after that he finished writing his last few works, then sadly spent all the later years of his long life as a recluse with no musical output at all.

After abandoning his life as a soldier in the Russian army, MODESTE MUSSORGSKY (1839–81) began to compose full time. He is one of the better-known members of the Russian group of composers known as the Mighty Handful (Rimsky-Korsakov, Borodin, Balakirev and Cui are the other members), who all held similar nationalistic views with respect to what music ought to be about. Two of his best-known works, which only achieved their great reputation due to later orchestrations by other composers, are *Pictures at an Exhibition,* orchestrated by Ravel (Dorati, Mercury 434 346-2), and *Night on the Bare Mountain,* orchestrated by Rimsky-Korsakov (Dorati, Mercury 432 004-2).

Perhaps the most poorly educated, yet most important of the Mighty Handful, NIKOLAI RIMSKY-KORSAKOV (1844–1908) had the greatest influence on Russian music for years to come. He was a teacher of Prokofiev and Stravinsky and his book on orchestration is still seen as one of the most important studies on the subject. His best-known piece is the symphonic suite *Scheherezade* (Bernstein, Sony SMK47605).

The output of GIACOMO PUCCINI (1858–1924) consists mainly of operatic works, some of which are still our most popular operas today. His most successful endeavours were *Tosca* (Karajan, Decca 421 670-2), *La Bohème* (Beecham, EMI mono CDS7 47235-8) and *Madame Butterfly* (Sinopoli, DG Dig. 423 567-2). When I was Prime Minister in 1972, I went on a visit to Japan and was taken on a tour of some monasteries. At one I heard a performance on ancient instruments that dated from AD 600. Later I went to lunch with the Emperor. In an alcove of the hall there were more of those ancient instruments, and the musicians began to play them. I told the Empress about my visit to the monasteries and asked her if she enjoyed this form of traditional Japanese music. 'Oh no,' she replied, 'I much prefer Puccini.' Today the appeal of his works is as great as ever. He is arguably the ultimate composer of Romantic opera.

GUSTAV MAHLER (1860–1911) wrote nine symphonies and numerous songs, which are now part of the regular programme of every orches-tra. This is in great contrast to Mahler's lifetime, for his career was beset by political intrigue and anti-Semitism, until his final, relatively happy period in the United States. By then he was already ill with the heart complaint that was to kill him. His First and Second symphonies were splendidly recorded by Bruno Walter in the late fifties and are still avail-able together in an excellent set (Sony SM2K 64447). Lenny Bernstein produced a whole series of fine Mahler recordings, including two full symphonic cycles, and some of his individual recordings are the very finest available (No. 3 with the New York PO, Sony M2YK 47576; No. 4 with the Concertgebouw, DG 423 607-2; No. 6 with the Vienna PO, DG 427 697-2; and No. 9 in a recording of the only occasion on which he conducted the Berlin PO, DG 435 378-2). Symphony No. 5 was famously recorded by Sir John Barbirolli (EMI CDM7 64749-2) and this remains an outstanding recording of this extremely difficult piece.

Gilbert Kaplan, financier and Mahler-expert, has recorded the Second Symphony, and the Adagietto of the Fifth Symphony, both with very favourable results. These performances are now available in a remarkable multi-media package, along with recordings of four of Mahler's own piano-roll performances and a CD-ROM of Mahler photographs (Conifer Classics 75605 51277 2). Apart from his symphonies, Mahler's *Das Lied von der Erde* (Walter, Ferrier, VPO, Decca mono 414 194-2) is a remarkable and truly moving work.

Not to be confused with the Austrian waltz-king Johann Strauss, the German RICHARD STRAUSS (1864–1949) is best known for his development and mastery of the tone poem, a form pioneered by Liszt. These include *Ein Heldenleben, Till Eulenspiegels lustige Streiche, Don Juan* and *Also sprach Zarathustra*. Rudolf Kempe recorded a complete set of the tone poems, and these stand among the best that exist today. Strauss also wrote ground-breaking operas such as *Der Rosenkavalier* (Schwarzkopf/Karajan, EMI CDS7 49354-8) and *Salome* (Sinopoli, DG Dig. 431 810-2). Several years ago I was given the final page of Act I from Strauss's original manuscript of *Der Rosenkavalier* and it is one of my most prized possessions.

CLAUDE DEBUSSY (1862–1918) was perhaps the most influential man in the movement of French Impressionism. Both Debussy and Ravel heard a Javanese gamelan orchestra at the Paris Exhibition in 1889 and could not help but be deeply influenced by what they heard. Debussy's most popular work for orchestra, *La Mer* (Solti, CSO, Decca 436 468-2), is the most passionate of musical representations of the sea. To me, this work and many of his others can be most simply described as 'refreshing'.

Another French Impressionist, MAURICE RAVEL (1875–1937), was responsible for creating a new form of piano technique and a distinctly new orchestral sound. Throughout his life he was constantly compared with Debussy, and their careers often ran parallel to each other. He composed many orchestral works including the ballet *Daphnis et Chloë* (Dutoit, 400 055-2), the Piano Concerto in G Major (Bernstein, Sony SMK47571) and much piano music.

Highly acclaimed as a conductor, and even more so as a pianist, SERGEI RACHMANINOV (1873–1943) is best remembered for his compositions for piano. Born in Russia, where his work was banned for some time, he later settled in America. Although he spent most of his later life touring as a pianist, his piano concerti, specifically the Piano Concerto No. 2 (Tirimo, Levi, CFP CD-CFP 9017), and his symphonies have guaranteed his works a permanent place in the canon of Western music. They usually contain strong Romantic sentiments, even though this style was becoming less and less fashionable as he was writing.

Also born in Russia, IGOR STRAVINSKY (1882–1972) later lived in France until finally settling in the United States. He is best known for his revolutionary ballets *The Rite of Spring* (Bernstein, NYPO, Sony SMK47629), *The Firebird* (LSO, Dorati, Mercury 432 012-2), and *Petroushka* (Bernstein, NYPO, Sony SMK47629). Today these works are almost always performed without choreography and contain some of the most challenging music (for the performer as well as the listener) written in the twentieth century.

Russian composer and pianist SERGEI PROKOFIEV (1891–1953) spent much time travelling around the United States and Europe before settling in Russia. His most productive period was in the time before he was living permanently there, for the Soviet government stifled his creative output for the remainder of his life. He wrote several immensely popular symphonies, of which Symphony No. 5 is the most memorable (Previn, LSO, EMI CDM 565 181-2), piano concerti, orchestral suites, a ballet score for *Romeo and Juliet* (vividly played by Georg Solti and the Chicago SO and paired with Symphony No. 1 on 430 731-2), and the light-hearted *Peter and the Wolf* with verbal commentary as well as the popular suite from his film-music, *Lieutenant Kijé* (Szell, Sony SBK48162).

The life and music of Russian composer DIMITRI SHOSTAKOVICH (1906–75) were constantly and inexorably tied to the state in which he lived. He was never fully embraced by the Communist regime, and much of his music is based on Russian folk tunes and is deeply rooted in the tradition of Russian composers. His sense of musical irony and occasional use of jazz idioms make Shostakovich stand apart from his fellow Russian contemporaries. His best-known work is the Symphony No. 5 (Rostropovich, DG 445 577-2), and other notable compositions include fourteen other symphonies, works for solo piano and two piano concerti, as well as a remarkable series of string quartets.

CHARLES IVES (1874–1954) was a tax accountant by day and a composer by night. His music often sounds experimental, as his techniques push the limits of aural tolerance at every opportunity. One of his more popular works is a musical description of the result of two marching bands playing different pieces at different tempos as they pass each other. After first becoming interested in Ives's music through hearing some of it on the radio, I rushed out and bought all the Ives recordings I could find, and have since developed quite an affinity for his music. His Symphony No. 3 (Bernstein, NYPO, Sony SMK47568) is one of my favourites and earned Ives a Pulitzer Prize in 1947. As an organist, I cannot help but be partial to his *Variations on 'America'* (Andrew Davis,

Carlton Classics, PCD 1082), even though I am quite sure that that tune was familiar somewhere before the Americans adopted it as their own.

LEONARD BERNSTEIN (1918–90) was one of the composers whom I knew best personally, and I shall always treasure memories of a friendship with an extraordinary man. He was unquestionably a genius, a brilliant composer as well as a fine pianist, and one of the greatest conductors of the century. Above all, however, he could really make music live, particularly for young people, through his lectures and teaching. Perhaps the best way of getting to know his music is through his own recordings of his two greatest stage works, *West Side Story* and the operetta *Candide,* which are available in a three-CD set from Deutsche Grammophon (DG 447 958-2). The rest of the DG Bernstein Edition is also worth exploring, in particular Lenny's own Vienna recording of his *Chichester Psalms,* written for England's Three Choirs Festival and including some of the most transcendentally beautiful music written in the second half of the twentieth century (DG 447 954-2).

Lenny Bernstein's close friend and teacher AARON COPLAND (1900–90) also wrote some of the most accessible and attractive music of the twentieth century. His ballet score *Appalachian Spring* (DG 413 324-2), written for the leading ballet impresaria Martha Graham, ends with a delightful treatment of an old Shaker tune better known in Britain as 'The Lord of the Dance' – and recordings conducted by Bernstein and Copland himself are eminently recommendable. For exquisite treatment of catchy folk tunes, Copland's *Old American Songs* is without peer, as is the recording of them by Thomas Hampson, with Dawn Upshaw singing Copland's Emily Dickinson songs (Teldec 9031-77310-2).

A member of the Second Viennese School, ALBAN BERG (1885–1935) is known for his use of serialism and the twelve-tone row. His controversial operas *Wozzeck* (Abbado, DG 423 587-2) and *Lulu* (Boulez, DG 415 489-23) and his Violin Concerto are notable for their deviations from conventional tonality and brought him constant streams of criticism. I quite enjoy his music and I have seen three productions of *Lulu*. The first occasion was the first performance of the three acts of *Lulu,* completed by Cerha. It was brilliantly performed in Paris under Pierre Boulez, the stage settings were absolutely appropriate, and it was played in the detailed way that Berg had written into the script. I regarded it as a huge success, and the recording I recommend was based upon that first-class production.

Over a decade later I saw a production at the Salzburg Festival, which completely ignored those instructions and Berg's interpretation of the script. Additionally the production paid no attention to the different settings that are required by the various emotions expressed during the action. Then in 1996 I saw another production at Glyndebourne, where everything was done with the same set. Some producers do not realize how infinitely boring it can become to an audience to look at the same set for three hours. They are also wasting countless opportunities that they could have used to bring out Berg's intentions by carrying out his clear instructions.

In recent years there has been a welcome return from the extremes of modernism in musical composition, which had threatened to turn modern music into a ghetto. Quite properly, composers continue to seek out new sound worlds and to experiment, but they seem to be sensitive again to the preferences and sensibilities of their audiences. It is difficult to guide people towards contemporary music, because buying it is always a gamble. However, readers might like to try the music of the Polish composer WITOLD LUTOSŁAWSKI (1913–94), which is always rhythmically vital and full of his distinctively fragmented melodies. There could not be a better introduction to his music than the pairing from Esa-Pekka Salonen of his Third and Fourth symphonies, played by the Los Angeles Philharmonic Orchestra on a Sony CD (SK 66280).

BRITISH MUSIC

HENRY PURCELL (1659–95) is widely perceived as England's first great musical talent. His operatic works, which brought him much acclaim, include *Dido and Aeneas* (Raymond Leppard, ECO, ERAT 2292-45263-2) and *The Fairy Queen* (performed with great style and aplomb under the direction of Benjamin Britten on Decca 433 163-2). As the composer for a number of members of the royal family, Purcell created a wide variety of anthems, fanfares and ceremonial music.

SIR EDWARD ELGAR (1857–1934) is often seen as the man responsible for rejuvenating the ailing British tradition of music. Largely self-taught, he was well known in his time, principally due to the popularity of his celebratory works such as the *Pomp and Circumstance* marches. Elgar was a prominent conductor, and his interpretations of his own works are yardsticks of authenticity. Most of his recordings are still available today, but as they were made in the late twenties and early thirties, the sound quality is, of course, not comparable to more recent recordings. There are excellent, mid-priced recordings on the Naxos label of both of his symphonies (Symphony No. 1 – Hurst, BBC PO, NAXO 8 550634; Symphony No. 2 – Downes, BBC PO, NAXO 8 550635). Probably his most noteworthy composition, the 'Enigma' Variations, has been recorded so often that selecting a single recommendation is virtually impossible – but I should not wish to be without the wisdom of Sir Adrian Boult with the LSO (EMI CDM7 64015-2).

Jacqueline Du Pré's celebrated rendering of the Elgar Cello Concerto is still the best recording (Barbirolli, EMI CDC7 47329-2), and I think that one of Nigel Kennedy's most successful endeavours was Elgar's Violin Concerto with the London Philharmonic Orchestra (EMI CD-EMX2058). Of Elgar's oratorios, I believe his most winning and moving is the *Dream of Gerontius,* never better performed than by another of our great composers, Benjamin Britten (Decca 448 170-2). Two of his others, *The Kingdom* (Boult, LPO, EMI CMS7 64209-2) and *The Apostles* (Boult, LPO, EMI CMS7 64206-2), are also very powerful works.

Perhaps my favourite of Elgar's compositions is his 'Cockaigne' Overture. I have now performed this work all over the world, and I think it really gives an accurate portrayal of London and its many bustling activities. This overture also represents a milestone in my life. As Prime Minister in 1971 I fulfilled a lifelong dream and conducted this piece with the London Symphony Orchestra. I remember that as André Previn was introducing it to the audience, he told them that since he had let me take over his orchestra for fifteen minutes, he ought to be able to take over Downing Street for the same length of time! I hope that the reader will forgive me for recommending the performance that means most to me – a live recording of that very concert (Heath, LSO, EMI 5 66063 2).

Earning his living as a professional trombonist, GUSTAV HOLST (1847–1934) only bloomed as a composer late in life. By far his most popular work is *The Planets* (Boult, EMI CDM7 64748-2), which thrust his name into national and international recognition. He is also responsible for a number of excellent works for wind band.

FREDERICK DELIUS (1862–1934) was born in Bradford into a merchant family, and decided at the age of twenty that he must make a career in

music. His music is still not particularly fashionable, but typifies for me
– just as much as that of Elgar – the pastoral style that English composers
of the twentieth century have maintained in the face of compositional
radicalism elsewhere in Europe. I am especially fond of the interlude
'The Walk to the Paradise Garden' from Delius's opera *A Village Romeo
and Juliet,* a piece included in a fine EMI collection of orchestral works
by Delius, played by the London Symphony Orchestra and conducted
by Sir John Barbirolli (CMS 565 119 2). There is also a splendid collection of orchestral works with Sir Thomas Beecham conducting his Royal
Philharmonic Orchestra, also on EMI (CDS 747 509 8). Both sets
include the hypnotically beautiful prelude to Delius's opera *Irmelin.*

Deeply immersed in the English folk-song tradition, RALPH VAUGHAN
WILLIAMS (1872–1958) spent much of his life furthering this aspect of
British music. He and his friend and contemporary, Gustav Holst, are
often seen as England's finest musical nationalists, and deservedly so.
His concerti and operas are eclipsed by his superior symphonies and
well-known orchestral and vocal works. I regret never conducting his
Symphony No. 1, the 'Sea Symphony', which was written using selected
texts from Walt Whitman's poetry. It is a splendid work that requires a
large chorus and orchestra and does not lend itself well to the efforts of
a guest conductor, which unfortunately is usually my role. There is a
splendid recording of this symphony by André Previn conducting the
London Symphony Orchestra (BMG/RCA GD 90500). Some of his
other excellent works, the Fantasia on 'Greensleeves', Fantasia on a
Theme by Thomas Tallis and 'The Lark Ascending', are all on a superb
CD with the London Chamber Orchestra directed by Christopher
Warren-Green (Virgin/EMI Dig. CUV5 61126-2).

Writing mainly in the neo-Romantic style, SIR WILLIAM WALTON

(1902–83) carried on the tradition of British music after Elgar. One of the finest evenings we had at No. 10 when I lived there was his seventieth birthday celebration. Some of the best-known names in British music, including Ben Britten, Yehudi Menuhin, Arthur Bliss, Georg Solti, Herbert Howells and Malcolm Arnold, were there to celebrate this great man's life. His notable works include *Façade, Belshazzar's Feast,* two symphonies (No. 1 – Previn, LSO, BMG/RCA GD87830; No. 2 – Szell, Cleveland, Sony SBK62753), viola and violin concerti (Nigel Kennedy, EMI CDC7 49628-2), and a number of scores for various Shakespeare films, two of which have been gloriously recorded with accompanying readings by Sir John Gielgud on the Chandos label: *Hamlet* (CHAN 8842) and *Richard III* (CHAN 8841).

Well known as a pianist, conductor and composer, BENJAMIN BRITTEN (1913–76) developed one of the most distinct voices in British music. His operas include *Peter Grimes* (Decca 414 577-2), *The Rape of Lucretia* (Decca 425 666-2) and his last large-scale work, *Death in Venice* (Decca 425 669-2). Two rather less well-known works are the Coronation opera, which Britten wrote for Queen Elizabeth II, *Gloriana,* and which was so triumphantly revived in 1995 by Opera North and recorded by the forces of the Welsh National Opera in a definitive performance (Charles Mackerras, Decca 440 213-2); and the extraordinary American folk operetta, *Paul Bunyan* (Virgin/EMI Dig. VCD7 59249-2).

Britten's non-operatic vocal works include the wonderful Serenade for Tenor, Horn and Strings (Britten, Pears, Brain, Decca 425-996-2) and the *War Requiem*. This was written for the opening of the new Coventry Cathedral, specifically to be performed by a Russian soprano (Galina Vishnevskaya, Rostropovich's wife), an English tenor (Peter Pears) and a German bass-baritone (Dietrich Fischer-Dieskau). This mix of soloists was to represent the three major warring countries in 'Europe in the twentieth century, which have now come to peace. Sadly, the Cold War prevented Galina Vishnevskaya from taking part in that première performance. She does, however, feature on the recording made shortly afterwards under the composer's own baton (Decca 414 383-2). The work is an excellent testimony to the peace that can be achieved in Europe in these modern times. Britten's best instrumental music consists of string quartets, songs and a witty, informative piece written primarily for young people *(The Young Person's Guide to the Orchestra,* Decca 436 990-2). Ben Britten and his lifelong associate, Peter Pears, came to Downing Street once, and I frequently attended the music festival that they founded in Aldeburgh, which today carries on as one of the finest international music festivals in the world.

The recording process has brought many first-rate performances into the home, and has provided both an alternative to concert-going and a means of augmenting it. Recordings will never wholly supplant the adrenalin and sense of occasion that come with live performances, but they are an invaluable way of both widening and deepening musical experience. With the proliferation of so many excellent new and reissued recordings available on CD for less than the price of a decent seat in a concert hall, recordings now – more than ever before – provide an appealing way of getting to know the repertoire through performances of the highest standard.

Some of my greatest pleasure from music has come from recordings, and I hope that some of my recommendations and reflections on these pages will prompt others to share in what I regard as one of humanity's greatest treasure troves: a century-long legacy of recorded music.

INDEX